Johannes Zachhuber
Time and Soul

CHRONOI
Zeit, Zeitempfinden, Zeitordnungen
Time, Time Awareness, Time Management

———

Herausgegeben von

Eva Cancik-Kirschbaum, Christoph Markschies
und Hermann Parzinger

Im Auftrag des Einstein Center Chronoi

Band 6

Johannes Zachhuber
Time and Soul

From Aristotle to St. Augustine

DE GRUYTER

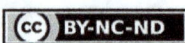

This work is licensed under the Creative Commons Attribution-NonCommercial-NoDerivatives 4.0 International License. For details go to http://creativecommons.org/licenses/by-nc-nd/4.0/.

ISBN 978-3-11-069272-3
e-ISBN (PDF) 978-3-11-069275-4
e-ISBN (EPUB) 978-3-11-069276-1
ISSN 2701-1453
DOI https://doi.org/10.1515/9783110692754

Library of Congress Control Number: 2022935637

Bibliographic information published by the Deutsche Nationalbibliothek
The Deutsche Nationalbibliothek lists this publication in the Deutsche Nationalbibliografie; detailed bibliographic data are available on the Internet at http://dnb.dnb.de.

© 2022 Johannes Zachhuber, published by Walter de Gruyter GmbH, Berlin/Boston
Printing and binding: CPI books GmbH, Leck

www.degruyter.com

For Katharina
8 March 1970 – 30 November 2021

Acknowledgements

This book would not exist were it not for the generosity of the Einstein Center Chronoi. It was there, during a yearlong fellowship in 2018–19, that I had the opportunity to research the connection of time and soul in the wake of Aristotle's *Physics*. I therefore express my heartfelt gratitude to everyone at this marvellous institution in leafy Berlin-Dahlem. I was made to feel welcome from the first day by its competent team led by Stefanie Rabe. The Center's directors, Eva Cancik-Kirschbaum, Christoph Markschies, and Hermann Partzinger are exemplary leaders and were inspirational conversation partners throughout my time as a fellow. I felt privileged to enjoy the company of the many other fellows whose time at the Chronoi overlapped with mine and who shared their own ideas and were willing to listen to mine.

At the Chronoi Center, I was given the opportunity to present some early ideas for the present book as a seminar paper. I am grateful to the participants, notably Glenn Most and Wolfgang Detel, for a stimulating discussion and constructive criticism which has helped me hone my argument.

By the time my fellowship came to its end, my ideas were ready, but they were not yet written down. I am therefore, as ever, grateful to Trinity College and the University of Oxford who supported my research after my return to my full-time academic role. This academic community proved its worth when, only few months after my return from Berlin, the Covid-19 pandemic broke out and altered the way everyone had to work. While the pandemic inevitably changed plans and slowed down my research on this book, it added a unique note to my own awareness of time.

I finalised the manuscript save for some editing in Paris. I owe this sojourn to my wife, Lydia Schumacher, who was elected a fellow of the Fondation Maison des Sciences de l'Homme and let me accompany her during her own stay last September. For this and for the many other things through which she sustains me daily in my life and work I am grateful to her.

The complete manuscript has benefited from the professional care of Gene Trabich who scrutinised the whole text and offered valuable advice on questions ranging from accessibility to style to linguistic correctness. Remaining mistakes, as always, are my own responsibility.

I dedicate the book to the memory of my sister, Katharina Zachhuber, who died too early on 30 November 2021. The enormous strength and courage she showed in the final years of her life and until her very last days, her love of life and her capacity for happiness in the face of terminal illness were an inspiration to all who knew her. As her life was nearing its end, she was able to savour the time that remained for her.

London, March 2022
Johannes Zachhuber

Contents

Introduction —— 1
    Cosmic time and human awareness of time —— 1
    Late ancient philosophy: schools of thought and the exegesis of classical texts —— 5
    From Aristotle to St. Augustine —— 7

1 Aristotle on Time and Soul —— 10
    Aristotle's philosophy of nature —— 10
    Time in Aristotle's *Physics* —— 11
    Aristotle's *aporia:* can time exist without soul? —— 16

2 Time and Soul in the Peripatetic Tradition —— 22
    Time without soul: Boethus of Sidon —— 22
    Alexander of Aphrodisias: commentator and philosopher —— 29
    Alexander on Aristotle's *aporia* —— 31
    Time and the cosmic soul —— 34
    The world soul prior to Alexander —— 36
    Alexander's contribution to the discussion about time and soul —— 40

3 Soul and Time in Neoplatonist Interpretations of Aristotle —— 47
    Plotinus on time and soul —— 49
    Plotinus on Aristotle's *aporia* —— 51
    Simplicius' Commentary on Aristotle's *Physics* —— 54
    Simplicius on Aristotle's *aporia* —— 56

4 Time and Soul in Patristic Thought —— 63
    John F. Callahan and the psychological theory of time —— 64
    Augustine on time as the distention of the spirit —— 68
    Augustine's theory of time and the universal soul —— 74
    Time and soul in Augustine: an assessment —— 79

Conclusion —— 82

Bibliography —— 87
    Primary Sources —— 87
    Secondary Literature —— 88

General Index —— 94

Index of Ancient Sources —— 97

Introduction

Cosmic time and human awareness of time

What is time? A first, intuitive answer may be that time is a dimension of the physical universe. As such, it exists and has always existed independently of human experience. We thus find it natural to assign temporal identities to events that took place millions of years before humanity even came into being, in particular in areas such as astrophysics, geology, and palaeontology. We know, or we think we know, that the universe came into existence with the Big Bang some 15 billion years ago, and with it space and time as we know it. Why time has existed in the particular way it has – notably as unidirectional – is still hard to understand, but the fact seems indisputable and is taken for granted in many facets of our daily lives. Time in this sense allows us to identify individual, non-repeatable moments in the past as well as the future, thus permitting universally valid statements to be made about the temporal sequence or the coincidence of events that take place in various parts of the world. Time thus understood establishes relationships between any two events that have ever taken place in the history of the world. In fact, we can say that it establishes such a thing as a 'history of the universe' in the first place.

While many of the ideas we today connect with physical time would have seemed strange to people in antiquity, the notion that time was an aspect of the physical world was widely shared. As such, it seemed most obviously connected with the regularities seen in astronomical observations: the daily and annual cycle of the sun; the waxing and waning of the moon; the movements of planets and of the fixed stars. Inevitably, these observations tended to suggest that time is cyclical, and involves the periodic return and recurrence of the same or similar events albeit with some variety at the level of individual being. Yet while ancient conceptions of physical time are thus far different from the linear models preferred in our own time, both share the underlying notion of time as a feature of the cosmos which we may observe or measure, but which exists independently of human perception let alone of human measurement.

It is arguable, however, that the notion of time as an objective aspect of the physical world is incomplete and possibly misleading. After all, it is difficult to think of or describe the reality of time in a way that does not include someone who is already aware of it. Time is not visible or material in the way the earth or the sun or even a single stone or an antelope is. Rather, it appears, time is inseparable from the mind that has consciousness of time. To us, at least, time seems ineluctably part of how we think and speak about the world, one way in which we order the things we experience as not only spatially arranged but also as occurring in a temporal sequence. Time, then, also has an experiential dimension. This aspect of time is often called subjective, but the use of this term is not without its problems. The point is not that, as we sometimes say, a particular hour to us seemed to 'last forever' or that our holidays were over 'in no time at all'. Rather, time in its physical reality, counted in seconds, minutes, hours, days, and years is tied to our own experience of reality as temporal leading to our consequent conceptualisation of the world in temporal terms.

This line of thought can be taken a step further to involve the claim that time is *primarily* an expression of human temporality. This claim was asserted with vigour in the twentieth century by Martin Heidegger who spoke of time as a human 'existential', one of the fundamental determinations of human existence and *as such* a basic category of ontology. For Heidegger, the scientific objectivity of reality, as expressed, for example, in chronological measurement was a derivative phenomenon which could and should never have been detached from its basis in existential experience.[1]

One of Heidegger's points of reference for this radical claim was an ancient author, Augustine of Hippo.[2] St. Augustine, undoubtedly one of the most influential thinkers in the entire history of Western philosophy, had a fascination for time that was arguably unparalleled in the whole of antiquity. Time to him seemed to be one of those realities that are at once self-evident and hard to explain: 'What is time? Provided that no one asks me, I know. If I want to explain it to an enquirer, I do not know.'[3] In his most sustained attempts at answering the question of what time is, Augustine, too, took his starting point from the subjective side of temporal experience. *For us* there is past, present, and future, and this structure from which our experience can never escape is the reason why to us the world seems inescapably temporal. In this sense, Augustine could define time as the *distentio animi*, the distention of the mind.[4] Time thus *was* primarily a property of our mind or soul which could not but consider the world as extended in past, present, and future. Augustine did not deny that time had an objective dimension, in fact, he was adamant that it was created by God together with the creation of the world,[5] and yet his deepest reflections about the nature

---

1 Heidegger 1927, § 81.
2 For a full account cf. Agustín Corti 2006.
3 Augustine, *Confessiones* XI 14, 17. ET: Chadwick 1991, 249.
4 *Ibid.* XI 26, 33.
5 Augustine, *Confessiones* XI 14, 17.

of time led him into the interior of the human mind, not to the observation of the cosmos.

In many ways, Augustine's theory of human temporality was novel in antiquity, but the underlying interest in subjective time was not quite unique. The question of whether time would exist if no one was conscious of it was raised in one of the most momentous texts in ancient philosophy, Aristotle's *Physics*.[6] Aristotle merely presented a question, an *aporia:* 'Someone might raise the puzzle whether if there were no soul there would be time or not.'[7] Through the ages, his readers have disagreed on almost every aspect of this question and the few subsequent lines in which Aristotle glossed it.

To begin with, they found it difficult to ascertain which answer to the *aporia* the Stagirite himself had in mind or was expecting his readers to infer from his text. Equally controversial has been the problem of whether Aristotle would have been right to postulate the existence of a soul that is aware of time in order for time to exist. At the same time, the mere fact that this *aporia* was included in the *Physics*, which already in late antiquity became a foundational text for the philosophy of nature, was sufficient for it to garner discussion over the centuries. These discussions which began among later Greek philosophers in the first centuries of the common era were continued among Islamic philosophers at the end of the first millennium and found new attention in the Western Middle Ages.[8]

The present book will mostly be an exploration of the first part of the conversation that ensued from attempts to understand Aristotle's *aporia*. As will become clear, Aristotle's readers in late antiquity focussed on a problem that all appeals to subjective time face: how can time be somehow dependent on the mind but also have intersubjective validity? In other words, provided we *do* accept that time cannot be understood apart from its existence in the mind, how can it still be the same for everybody? At this point, interest in Aristotle's *aporia* coincided with another intellectual trajectory flowing, this time, from Plato's late dialogue *Timaeus*. The *Timaeus* was Plato's account of the creation of the world. In this text, he had argued that the world as a whole was comparable to a living being and, for that reason, not only had a body but also a soul.[9]

The idea of a world soul, which took its beginning from this text, proved inspiring and became a fixture in later ancient debates about cosmology. To some of those who found in Aristotle's *Physics* a hint that time could not exist without

---

6 Aristotle, *Physics* IV 14 (223a21–9).
7 *Ibid.* ET: Coope 2005, 159.
8 For the fullest presentation of this discussion cf. Jeck 1994.
9 Plato, *Timaeus* 30b4-c1 (the world as a living being) and 34a-b for the creation of the world soul.

a mental foundation, it therefore seemed plausible to defend this statement by applying it to this entity. Even in Augustine, who had theological reasons to be wary of a world soul, we find traces of this idea.

The purpose of the present book is to examine the history of these various attempts. It thus presents the story of time and soul in antiquity, but this story is here investigated almost exclusively through the lens of the reception of Aristotle's *aporia*. Only the final chapter, which deals with some early Christian authors, will decisively break with this methodological restriction in order to show how the problem of cosmic and experiential time received a new form within the theistic framework imposed by the new religion of late antiquity.

Woven into this story are elements of the reception of Plato's theory of the world soul among Stoics, Peripatetics, Neoplatonists, and the early Christians. The book will thus describe an interference of traditions which are often still considered mutually exclusive. This is as true for the relationship between Platonic and Aristotelian cosmologies as it is for the overall contrast between these philosophical schools on the one hand and early Christian theologies on the other. As the detailed account will show, however, these oppositions, while not without a basis in our sources, cannot be taken as absolutes.

The history recounted in the following pages may appear like recalling some rather obscure and potentially implausible ideas remote from today's conceptions about either time or the physical universe. To address Aristotle's query with the help of a Platonic theory we know Aristotle rejected, may moreover seem to make a conceptual muddle worse without assisting either the interpretation of the Stagirite's text or the clarification of the problem. And yet, such a conclusion may prove rash. If we accept that the underlying problem is the subjective, experiential dimension of time, its location in the world soul reveals the paradoxical nature of such a quest. After all, the world soul, in Platonic cosmology, is itself a cosmic entity. If it can explain the existence of time, the 'time' it constitutes would be as much cosmic and 'objective' as it would be 'subjective' and experiential. In other words, the solution these late ancient thinkers were gesturing at in their interpretation of Aristotle's *aporia* was one in which the duality of objective and subjective time was no longer a dichotomy. In fact, in some of the more Platonic solutions, the objective element became so strong that the subjective dimension of time seems absent even though time is associated with the soul.

Late ancient philosophy: schools of thought and the exegesis of classical texts

With the exception of Aristotle, Plotinus, and Augustine, none of the thinkers that will be discussed in what follows are individually famous for their part in the history of philosophy. It is possible to have studied philosophy, even ancient philosophy, for a long time without necessarily encountering their names. As a matter of fact, even in antiquity, they were not necessarily rated for their personal genius although they all were admired for their insights and were continually discussed. To explain their significance, it is necessary to say a few words at this point about the mode in which philosophy was mostly practiced during the centuries we today call late antiquity. I have in mind, broadly speaking, the time from the first century BCE to the sixth century CE. Inevitably, much changed during this period which, we must recall, encompasses over half a millennium.

Yet there are important continuities as well. Perhaps the most important one is that philosophy was mostly practiced in schools.[10] Being a philosopher principally meant to accept such a school as the authoritative context in which reflection on philosophical questions occurred. This implied that reading and trying to understand a canon of existing writings was a key component of philosophical work. It was philosophising through engagement with classic texts. This engagement was increasingly formalised resulting in the composition of line-by-line commentaries on the most important of these texts.[11]

Such an approach to the practice of philosophy inevitably minimised the significance of the philosopher as an individual. While their intellectual prowess was recognised and celebrated, it found its expression not in the creation of a novel system or in revolutionary transformations of traditionally accepted insights, but the refinement and the cultivation of a tradition. That many of the most important participants in this centuries-long philosophical development are little known to us in terms of their personal lives is therefore neither an indication of their lack of significance nor an historical accident but a consequence of their self-effacing approach to their work.

The same can be said about their writings. Insofar as the main product of creative intellectual work was the commentary on an established, classic text, its purpose was to be used and, so to speak, superseded by subsequent generations of those engaged in the same pursuit. The fact that some of the most influential and respected commentaries are no longer extant is testimony to this

---

[10] Hadot 2004, 97–102.
[11] Betegh 2010.

principle. Later authors used and excerpted them. For us, whose concern inevitably is the reconstruction of the original voice of individual authors from the period, this means that later, extant texts must be mined for their citations of earlier authors. As we shall see, this is emphatically the case for the present enquiry. Yet in some ways such an approach defies the logic of the historical process of tradition in which the intention of those partaking in it saw their own role as the increasing perfection of a growing body of interpretation rather than the presentation of their individual viewpoint.

One major change that occurred in the world of the philosophical schools from the third century onwards concerned the gradual disappearance of their plurality, which had been characteristic of the Hellenistic and early imperial period. The competition and frequent polemic between Epicureans, Stoics, Peripatetics, Platonists and some others increasingly gave way to a more integrated vision facilitated by the emergence of what we now call Neoplatonism, a version of Platonism keen to integrate the insights of other traditions, notably the Stoic and Peripatetic ones. What precisely drove this development is a complex question and may have to do with the growing sense that with the rise of Christianity as a radical alternative to existing schools their traditional differences had become less decisive than their commonalities.[12]

In scholarly terms, this development necessitated an even more synthetic approach to the interpretation of classic texts. This approach has often been caricatured in terms of the notion that for late ancient commentators Plato and Aristotle were 'in agreement'. Insofar as it seems clear that Aristotle's philosophy was, in many ways, written to counter some of Plato's key teachings, this diagnosis seemed to evidence the intellectual decline of an age that has often been associated with a process of cultural degeneration and even disintegration.

There are, however, several reasons to be critical of such a simple assessment.[13] For one, historians of ideas know that agreement and disagreement are often more relative than absolute terms. What can appear as the sharpest possible dissent within one conceptual framework, can reveal remarkable similarities when recontextualised. That from the perspective of half a millennium later, commonalities between the thinkers of the classical period came into view can be appreciated as a sensible premise without necessarily endorsing every single interpretative attempt at harmonising their ideas. Moreover, the sheer sophistication of philosophical reflection that was accomplished by Neoplatonist philosophers between the third and the sixth centuries, which more re-

---

12 Cf. Barney 2009, 104 who makes this point for Simplicius.
13 Cf. Karamanolis 2006; Barney 2009.

cent research has brought into sharp relief, defies the traditional classification of that period as philosophically unoriginal or barren.

Such a reassessment, on which recent research is mostly agreed, helps explain what otherwise must appear puzzling: the philosophers of the late ancient period were crucial for all major receptions of ancient philosophy. They were major sources for the Arabic reception and transformation of Greek thought, and they were equally important for the later Western appropriation of the same sources until at least the early nineteenth century.

The two facets of this historical process highlighted above, namely, the self-effacing character of work within the schools and the increasing tendency to strive towards a synthetic interpretation of the major classical texts, are foundational for much of the history that will be recounted in the present book. What will here be treated as individual viewpoints, assigned *faute de mieux* to little-known thinkers, is really the story of an interpretative tradition within which a certain exegetical problem was considered from various sides, contextualised and recontextualised within a growing corpus of classical texts. It is this *story* that, I would argue, can claim interest as much as it reports a diachronic attempt to unearth as much meaningful potential as possible from an authoritative source text. In the course of this history, as we shall see, some fascinating and truly relevant questions about the relationship between 'objective' and 'subjective' time will be the object of remarkably subtle philosophical reflection.

From Aristotle to St. Augustine

The historical arc of the present study is described in its subtitle as extending from Aristotle to St. Augustine. In purely chronological terms, the last author to be discussed will be the Neoplatonist Simplicius who lived a century after the Bishop of Hippo. Still, the Athenian philosopher and the Christian bishop appropriately describe the trajectory of the present narrative.

Its starting point should not be controversial. After all, the main topic of the book is the reception and discussion of a passage in Aristotle's *Physics*. Moreover, there is no disagreement on the fact that the Stagirite was historically the first Greek thinker to develop a full theory of time despite the fact that Plato and even some Presocratics had already formulated ideas about time which subsequently continued to be discussed. In many ways, Western philosophical reflection about time begins with the *Physics,* and for the remainder of antiquity at least there is no doubt that it continues to stand in the long shadow cast by this book.

Subsequent history most obviously flows through the Hellenistic schools, especially the Peripatetic school, to the Neoplatonic commentators of the later centuries of the common era. This continuity finds its most obvious expression in the existence of writings directly interacting with Aristotle's text resulting, from the second century onwards, in the production of full commentaries. By contrast, the relationship between the Aristotelian tradition and early Christian thought seems less self-evident. Early Christian writers rarely refer to Aristotle, and when they do, their references are usually so generic that their familiarity with a specific text cannot easily be gauged. Moreover, their attitude towards the Stagirite is usually critical or even hostile.[14] The endpoint of the history in patristic authors, notably in St. Augustine, therefore, needs a word of justification.

A famous mid-century book referred to St. Augustine as standing at the 'end of ancient culture'.[15] What the author, Henri-Irenée Marrou, had in mind was that the Bishop of Hippo could be seen as someone who, while in full possession of traditional ancient education, nevertheless was the first person who could imagine himself as standing outside this context. Thus far, Augustine was placed between the old and the new uniquely positioned as an end as well as a beginning. One does not fully have to commit to Marrou's analysis to see how this perspective makes sense of Augustine's place at the end of the story narrated in this book.

What I mean is that all the reasons that make Augustine stand apart from the main story pursued throughout the book also make him a fascinating thinker to be included here. In other words, the absence, by and large, of the kind of commitment described above to the interpretative tradition within a philosophical school and his resulting intellectual *liberty* in using earlier ideas as he saw fit, ensure for him a place at the conclusion of the present history which also gestures at its openness for subsequent developments.

The rise of Christianity is sometimes considered as a narrowing of the horizons in late antiquity symbolised by the censure of opinions that were at variance with an institutionalised faith which, from the late fourth century at least, allied itself with the political authority in such a way as to ensure that deviant viewpoints would be systematically excluded. The present account, without denying that novel intellectual constraints were introduced during those centuries, will nevertheless suggest that the whole story was more complex.

---

14 Cf. Edwards 2019 for a full discussion.
15 Marrou 1958.

There is no doubt that alongside Augustine's independence vis-a-vis the classical philosophical tradition stood his own commitment to the cause of Christianity. With regard to the topic of time, however, which was not in any obvious way defined by the teachings of his Church, Augustine clearly relished the originality of his own reflections. Thus, the bishop's reflections on time and soul show that Christian thinkers enjoyed a novel kind of freedom towards the theories inherited from the classical period and that this freedom *could* generate conceptual innovations which prepared the ground for later intellectual developments.

1 Aristotle on Time and Soul

Aristotle's philosophy of nature

While it is difficult to identify a beginning of human interest in the nature of time, the first systematic, philosophical treatment of the topic in the Western tradition was offered by Aristotle. His view is presented in Book IV of his *Physics*.[1] As all of Aristotle's extant works, the *Physics* was not a book prepared for publication, but a series of lectures given in Aristotle's school, the *Lyceum*, which he founded after breaking away from the Academy, the school of his teacher, Plato.[2]

Lecturing on *Physics*, Aristotle picked up a topic that had been central to the earliest phase of Greek philosophy many of whose representatives are reported to have written works *Peri physeos, On Nature*.[3] The Greek word *physis* is unusual in that it has no direct equivalents in most languages. English, and other modern Western languages, use either a term directly derived from the Greek, as in physics or physical for example, or they employ variants of the Latin term *natura*, which however was a rather artificial attempt by early Roman recipients of Greek thought to coin a term for the purposes of translating Greek philosophy.

What is unique about *physis* is that it means both the true being of a thing (as we would still say, its 'nature') and its origin.[4] Speaking of *physis*, then, suggests that we understand things in their innermost character by thinking of them in and through the process of their generation. *Physis*-language implies a view of the world which is at once dynamic and immanent. The world can be understood in and of itself, but this is no positivist reductionism but, rather, involves the perception of things as transparent for their true being as it shows itself in and through their changing appearance.

This view of the world was radically challenged by Parmenides who sharply contrasted true being with the realm of change and transition. Nature to him is part of the false reality of 'opinion' which the philosopher is called to avoid.[5]

---

1 Aristotle, *Physics* IV 10 – 14. This text has recently received considerable scholarly attention, cf. Coope 2005; Roark 2013; Harry 2015; Detel 2021.
2 I do not here address the complicated question, much discussed even among Aristotle's ancient readers, of whether the current *Physics* constitutes a unity or not. Cf. Harry, xvi-xvii, no. 8.
3 For what follows cf. Zachhuber 2016.
4 For the former meaning cf. Homer, *Odyssey* X 303; for the latter cf. Empedocles, *fr.* B 8 (Diels/Kranz).
5 Parmenides, *fr.* B 4, 5 – 8 (Diels/Kranz); B 10, 1 – 2 (Diels/Kranz). Cf. Curd 1998, 24 – 63. For an overview of more recent interpretations of Parmenides' philosophy see also: Palmer 2020.

True being, he held, can only be ascertained by emphasising permanence and immutability, properties absent from the world of our experience. Parmenides' critique of the older philosophy of nature was largely shared by Plato in whose writings, therefore, the term *physis* is restricted to the margins.[6] All the more significant is the fact that Aristotle brings the term and the project of natural philosophy back to prominence.

In doing so, Aristotle was far from simply renewing the older philosophy of nature.[7] Yet in one important regard he agreed with it against the towering figure of his erstwhile teacher. Explaining the world as we perceive it by reference to a transcendent reality which is fundamentally different from it seemed, to the Stagirite, an effort doomed to failure. Instead, we understand the physical world by seeking to comprehend it on its own terms. If it is changing, then the philosopher has to study change and explain how it is (and has to be) a constituent part of reality.

Aristotle's famous solution to this task lay in his metaphysical distinction between form and matter. The things that make up the world of our experience each consist of these two principles, and it is their tensional unity that explains that and how they change: their 'matter' represents the point of origin of their development (its 'potential') while their form determines its goal (its 'actuality'). This dual composition of the things of our reality, or *hylomorphism* to use the technical term, introduces into Aristotle's thought both a dynamic element and a principle of goal-directedness or teleology. Change in nature is not random but can be understood within the parameters of the natural movement from potentiality to actuality.

Time in Aristotle's *Physics*

Change, then, and movement are fundamental categories of Aristotle's *Physics*. To understand the natural world is to understand the way it changes and develops, constantly actualising its potentialities. It is, therefore, hardly surprising that Aristotle's interest in time is inscribed into this broader logic.[8] Time is a topic of the *Physics* insofar as change occurs in time. Time, thus far, is closely related to change. It therefore must be understood in this connection. This start-

---

6 For the critique of natural philosophy: Plato, *Phaedo* 95b-102a and *Laws* X 892c. Cf. however *Republic* X 597d for God as φυτούργος.
7 Bostock 2006, 1–18.
8 Harry 2015, xvii-xviii; Coope 2005, 2–3.

ing point indicates that Aristotle's theory of time, as so many other parts of his philosophy, was designed to counter views associated with Plato.

While the latter had not developed a detailed theory of time, he did refer to it as the 'moving image of eternity'.[9] For Plato, then, time was derivative reality. It was characteristic of the physical world because that world lacked the ontological perfection true being possessed. And yet, it was not entirely detached from that perfection. The *Timaeus*, Plato's major cosmological text, ascribes the origin of the physical world to a good Craftsman who competently modelled the cosmos on the paradigm of eternal forms. The world thus is not bad; in fact, it is *as perfect as possible*. This is true for time as well: it is *an image* (not a perversion) of eternity.[10] We best understand its nature by considering it vis-a-vis its archetype, and this is feasible, presumably, because it mirrors that archetype as nearly as possible under the conditions of physical existence.

Aristotle, however, did not think that such an approach could work. We have as little a grasp of what time is from a reflection on something that is essentially atemporal as we have an understanding of empirical reality on the basis of transcendent forms. A theory of time, rather, has to be developed out of reality as we observe it and thus, *nolens volens*, out of *changeable* reality.

At the same time, Aristotle did not simply identify time with change. In fact, such an identification seems to have been associated with members of Plato's academy.[11] Plato himself called time 'the wandering of the heavenly bodies' although this may not have been his considered view.[12] Aristotle, by contrast, introduced a distinction which stands at the heart of his account of time: time is not change or movement but rather 'something of change'.[13] In other words, while time is closely related to movement, the two cannot simply be identified. Aristotle's theory, then, can be said to consist of two conceptual decisions: on the one hand he aligned time with change while on the other hand maintaining it as a different reality. Attempts to understand his teaching can, in many ways, be classified based on how they balance these two tenets.

---

9 Plato, *Timaeus* 37d5.
10 As we shall see later, this is somewhat different for Plotinus who perceived more strongly the tragic dimension of human temporality.
11 (Ps.-)Plato, *Definitions* 411b: Time is 'the motion of the sun'. Cf. Coope 2005, 32.
12 Plato, *Timaeus* 39d. Cf. Coope, *ibid*.
13 Aristotle, *Physics* IV 11 (219a8–10): ὥστε ἤτοι κίνησις ἢ τῆς κινήσεώς τί ἐστιν ὁ χρόνος. ἐπεὶ οὖν οὐ κίνησις, ἀνάγκη τῆς κινήσεώς τι εἶναι αὐτόν. Cf. Coope 2005, 31–43. In using the somewhat clunky English phrase 'something of change', I follow Coope. Hussey 1983 (ad. loc.) translates 'some aspect of change', but as Coope rightly observes this can make it sound as if time is a property of change (2005, 31 n. 1).

As for the former, it is evident that much of Aristotle's argument in the relevant chapters of Book IV of his *Physics* is devoted to this line of argument. He introduces further concepts, magnitude, and continuity, to explain how change occurs in both space and time – and in both continuously – but also *needs* both dimensions to be explained.[14] Of particular importance in this connection is, Aristotle argues, a structure he calls the 'before and after'.[15] Change in space, he tells us, always involves this structure; we cannot even conceptualise change without thinking of it as the contrast between how something was 'before' and how it is 'afterwards'. In precisely the same way, he thinks, time is also inscribed into a 'before' and 'after' (τὸ πρότερον καὶ ὕστερον). As long as we do not apply this structure because, for example, we might experience an extended moment as somehow a continued present, 'no time seems to have passed'.[16] We only speak of time when we make the distinction between before and after thinking of the 'now' as 'bounded' or 'marked off' by these two limitations.[17]

This line of argument has engendered much criticism especially as it seems unclear how Aristotle can explain on this basis why time moves in solely one direction whereas change in space seems to permit for more than one direction.[18] More important for my present purpose, however, is the realisation that Aristotle here already sets himself up for the kind of question we shall discuss in more detail later on. Note how his insistence on the 'before' and 'after' and the dependence of time on the experience of a 'now' bounded by these two limits pivots his theory into a more subjective direction. In order to define what time is, Aristotle cannot only rely – or at least he does not only rely – on the physical reality of change. Rather, he appeals to *our own* awareness of time alongside its basis in nature.

There is little doubt that his reference to the triad of before, now, and after, refers to the structure of human awareness of time as past, present, and future. Even where Aristotle seems to develop his conception of time in a strictly physical context, he already introduces a concept that ties cosmic time to its mental presence:

> We mark off these [the before and after in change] by taking them to be different from each other, and some third thing between them. For whenever we think of the extremes as differ-

---

14 Aristotle, *Physics* IV 11 (219a14–21). Cf. for a full interpretation of these difficult lines: Coope 2005, 47–59.
15 Aristotle, *Physics* IV 11 (219a15). Cf. Coope 2005, 60–81.
16 Aristotle, *Physics* IV 11 (219a32–3): οὐ δοκεῖ χρόνος γεγονέναι οὐδείς.
17 Coope 2005, 85–6.
18 Coope 2005, 69–70.

ent from the middle and the soul says that the nows are two, one before and one after, then it is and this it is that we say time is.[19]

Throughout this passage, Aristotle uses the first-person plural to indicate commonly shared experience: 'we' mark off; 'we' conceive of before and after as other than the 'middle', i.e. the 'now'; 'the soul' counts the nows. The final statement here leads directly to Aristotle's famed definition of time as 'a number of change in respect of the before and after.'[20] In order to determine time, in other words, Aristotle appeals to an activity of the soul which counts 'nows', or individual, discrete moments of time, by being aware of them as distinct, in each case, from a preceding and a subsequent moment.

Once again, Aristotle's account poses serious problems not least the question, debated since antiquity, of how time can be a 'number' if it is continuous.[21] Scholars have also disagreed on whether 'number' simply means 'measure' or whether there is a difference between the two.[22] None of these problems can be discussed let alone settled in the present place. What matters is this: as much as Aristotle reiterates the necessity of the connection of time with change and space, he is equally adamant that, in order to understand what time is, the establishment of its physical basis is not sufficient. Rather, time is defined as a unique way in which we organise or structure our experience of change in the world by counting or numbering moments which we experience as bounded by before and after.

There is, then, a tension in Aristotle's theory as it holds together the physical character of time with the necessity of its mental appropriation. It has been suggested that this tension can, in theory, be resolved in four different ways:[23]

(1) A physicalist theory that closely aligns time and change;
(2) An idealist interpretation that makes time a construct of the mind;
(3) An intermediate position close to (1): time is physical but *discovered* by the mind

---

19 Aristotle, *Physics* IV 11 (219a26–9). ET: Coope 2005, 85: ὅταν γὰρ ἕτερα τὰ ἄκρα τοῦ μέσου νοήσωμεν, καὶ δύο εἴπῃ ἡ ψυχὴ τὰ νῦν, τὸ μὲν πρότερον τὸ δ' ὕστερον, τότε καὶ τοῦτό φαμεν εἶναι χρόνον· τὸ γὰρ ὁριζόμενον τῷ νῦν χρόνος εἶναι δοκεῖ.
20 Aristotle, *Physics* IV 11 (219b1–2) ET: Hussey 1983, 44: τοῦτο γάρ ἐστιν ὁ χρόνος, ἀριθμὸς κινήσεως κατὰ τὸ πρότερον καὶ ὕστερον.
21 Annas 1975, 107–13; Rashed 2011, 68; Coope 2005, 88.
22 Cf. Coope 2005, 96–8 for a full discussion of this question.
23 Rashed 2011, 58–9. The argument partly rests on the analogy between time and mathematical entities for which see also Annas 1975.

(4) An intermediate position close to (2): time is produced by the mind interacting with nature.

The two extreme positions are difficult to reconcile with the textual evidence as Aristotle clearly seeks to hold the two principles in tension. Time as 'something of change' cannot be fully understood without either the physical reality of change *or* the operation of the mind. As for the two intermediate positions, a decision between them may turn on Aristotle's distinction between the number that counts and the number that is counted.[24] According to Aristotle, time is number in the latter sense. Whatever the precise force of the distinction, it seems to move time as close to physical reality as is possible without identifying the two. Thus, Aristotle's view would seem closest to interpretation (3) above. In other words, he wants to ensure that time remains anchored in the things that change rather than drifting too far towards an ideal entity that is mainly part of our mental apparatus for dealing with the world.

To sum up, Aristotle approaches time within the context of his *Physics* to indicate that it has to be approached as part of the study of the empirical world. This world changes, and one of the ways in which this shows itself is the passage of time. In that sense, time is intimately related to change. At the same time, the definition of time as the 'number of change' indicates that time is not simply the same as change. Change, we might say, is proto-temporal; it has the before-and-after structure that also defines time. Nevertheless, time depends on a perception of change that is capable of identifying individual moments, 'nows', in the flux of the temporal continuum and of counting them, thus establishing them as an ordered series.[25]

If we consider Aristotle's theory of time in this tensional unity between its physical and mental dimensions, we see that his account, despite its overall tendency to align time with physical reality, also contains hints towards the notion of time as fundamentally dependent on the mind. The *aporia* Aristotle raises towards the end of his short treatise, thus, comes as less a surprise than it has sometimes seemed to his readers. It is now time to move on and consider this passage in more detail.

---

24 Aristotle, *Physics* IV 11 (219b6–8).
25 Cf. Harry 2015, xviii for the view that change is *potentially* time and has to be actualised by the mind.

Aristotle's *aporia:* can time exist without soul?

Aristotle's puzzle, which will stand at the centre of the remainder of this book, is found in the final section of his treatise on time (*Physics* IV 14). As we shall see, the problem the Stagirite raised there was the subject of debate throughout antiquity. Philosophical interest in the passage subsequently continued among Arabic and medieval Latin authors.[26] In the twentieth century, Martin Heidegger found in this text an early anticipation of his own understanding of human temporality.[27] There is no doubt that the text raises more questions than it answers, and it was arguably this very fact that has prompted the continuing debate among interpreters.

In recent research on Aristotle's theory of time, this passage has been variously treated. While Tony Roarke does not discuss it at all, the link between time and the soul is of great importance in Chelsey Harry's attempt to ascribe to Aristotle a view of time that is 'taken' by individual living beings.[28] This has led one of her critics, António Pedro Mesquita, to refute her overall thesis by denying that Aristotle even believed in the mutual dependence of time and soul.[29] Ursula Coope, in the most thoroughgoing treatment of *Physics* IV 10–14, however, has convincingly refuted the latter contention and shown how closely related time and soul are throughout Aristotle's entire treatment of it.[30]

The passage itself is brief. In English translation it runs as follows:

> Someone might raise the puzzle whether if there were no soul there would be time or not. For if it is impossible for there to be something to do the counting, it is impossible also that anything should be countable, so that it is clear that there will not be number. For number is either the counted or the countable. But if nothing else has the nature to count than soul (and in the soul, the intellect), it is impossible for there to be time if there is no soul, except that there could be that, whatever it is, by being which time is, for example, if it is possible for there to be change without soul. The before and after are in change and time is these in so far as they are countable.[31]

---

[26] Jeck 1994.
[27] Simesen de Bielke 2017.
[28] Roark 2013; Harry 2015, 56–61.
[29] Mesquita 2018, 465–6.
[30] Coope 2005, 159–72. Cf. also Jeck 1994, 6–13; Striowski 2016.
[31] Aristotle, *Physics* IV 14 (223a21–8). ET: Coope 2015, 159: πότερον δὲ μὴ οὔσης ψυχῆς εἴη ἂν ὁ χρόνος ἢ οὔ, ἀπορήσειεν ἄν τις. ἀδυνάτου γὰρ ὄντος εἶναι τοῦ ἀριθμήσοντος ἀδύνατον καὶ ἀριθμητόν τι εἶναι, ὥστε δῆλον ὅτι οὐδ' ἀριθμός. ἀριθμὸς γὰρ ἢ τὸ ἠριθμημένον ἢ τὸ ἀριθμητόν. εἰ δὲ μηδὲν ἄλλο πέφυκεν ἀριθμεῖν ἢ ψυχὴ καὶ ψυχῆς νοῦς, ἀδύνατον εἶναι χρόνον ψυχῆς μὴ οὔσης, ἀλλ' ἢ τοῦτο ὅ ποτε ὂν ἔστιν ὁ χρόνος, οἷον εἰ ἐνδέχεται κίνησιν εἶναι ἄνευ ψυχῆς. τὸ δὲ πρότερον καὶ ὕστερον ἐν κινήσει ἐστίν· χρόνος δὲ ταῦτ' ἐστὶν ᾗ ἀριθμητά ἐστιν.

To begin with, the passage clearly takes its starting point from Aristotle's definition of time as 'a number of change in respect to the before and after' (219b1–2). Insofar as this definition relies on the idea that time is counted, it seems to imply that there is someone who does the counting. Yet only souls count; more precisely, as Aristotle adds, only the intellect. Time therefore depends on the existence of soul and intellect.

A first question concerns what answer, if any, Aristotle intends the reader to infer from the puzzle. Some commentators have sought to deny that Aristotle thought that the premise of his reflection was valid.[32] After all, they urged, Aristotle introduced the passage in a way that only indicates that this is a problem deserving of an answer. His own answer, these readers observed, is not made explicit in the text, and it is therefore perfectly possible that Aristotle wanted readers to understand that, on the basis of his own philosophy of time, the solution had to be that time was *not* in fact dependent on soul.

This suggestion should, however, be dismissed. As we have seen, the notion that time and soul are interconnected is deeply rooted in the main body of Aristotle's treatise on time. It is therefore quite natural to read Aristotle as conceding that, following his own previous disquisition, the existence of time presupposes soul and, more specifically, a rational soul. The *puzzle* then is how this is possible and what it means for the natural world more broadly. To this puzzle, Aristotle not only gives no answer; he does not even, in the present place, provide any hints as to the kind of answer he deems appropriate.

Entirely open-ended seems to be a second question that is, so to speak, tacked on to the principal *aporia*, namely, whether change (i.e. that 'by being which time is'[33]) could exist without time. Aristotle seems to suggest that this might be possible insofar as time as number is different from change. *Prima facie*, therefore, two interpretations would seem feasible. Aristotle, it seems, believes either (1) that time cannot exist without soul, but change can; or (2) that ultimately neither time nor change exists without soul.

Richard Sorabji begins his discussion of this text in *Time, Creation, and the Continuum* with the question of whether Aristotle had simply made 'a silly mistake' here?[34] Ultimately, Sorabji does not think it was a 'silly' mistake although he does believe Aristotle was wrong to think that time required a soul that counts it. But why would it be a 'silly' mistake? Such a conclusion would appear to fol-

---

32 Coope 2015, 160. Those interpreters include Thomas Aquinas and, more recently, André-Jean Festugière and Victor Goldschmidt.
33 This is normally taken to be change although Aristotle subsequently seems to give 'change' as a possible example.
34 Sorabji 1983, 90.

low from a mostly 'objective' reading of Aristotle's theory. If the thrust of his account is seen in the establishment of time as a necessary feature of the natural world in its state of permanent change, it makes little sense to make time dependent on consciousness. On this kind of interpretation, calling time a number does as little to change its status as the observation that other natural things are countable. As one later reader noted, 'nothing prevents that something countable exists without someone counting as much as the perceptible exists without someone perceiving'.[35]

Against such an interpretation of Aristotle's theory, however, it needs to be recalled how strong the Stagirite's emphasis on the intellectual nature of time had been throughout his entire treatise. As Ursula Coope has argued, it therefore makes good sense to believe that Aristotle himself thought that time did not, and could not, exist without soul:

> Time, for Aristotle, is not an entity that is already there as a uniform continuum prior to our counting. On Aristotle's view, the unity of time depends upon our counting. By our counting we do indeed create potential divisions and the change-parts that they delimit, but it is only because we create these change-parts that changes can all be arranged in a single before and after order.[36]

Thus far, Coope argues, time is different from motion and change which do not depend in their existence on the soul's counting.[37] This does not mean, according to her, that Aristotle envisaged a possible world in which, hypothetically, change existed but no time. No such world, she suggests, could exist for the Stagirite who 'has the (to us strange) view that it is impossible for there to be a world without ensouled beings'.[38] Yet motion and change can be conceptualised without reference to a soul, whereas the same was not true for time.

In sum, Coope understands Aristotle as accepting the co-dependence of time and soul. Time as 'number' is essentially connected with the rational subject that imposes this structure on the underlying motion. Without this activity, time truly does not exist. The same, she insists, is not the case for motion and change. In this sense, she understands Aristotle's comment 'if it is possible for there to be change without soul' as expressing a theoretical possibility albeit one that could never be actualised as in Aristotelian physics the existence of ensouled beings was necessary.

---

35 Chiaradonna/Rashed 2020, 63 (fr. 37b): μηδὲν κωλύειν τὸ ἀριθμητὸν εἶναι καὶ δίχα τοῦ ἀριθμοῦντος, ὥσπερ καὶ τὸ αἰσθητὸν δίχα τοῦ αἰσθανομένου. Further on this text see below.
36 Coope 2005, 170–1.
37 Coope 2005, 161–3.
38 Coope 2005, 161.

Perhaps Coope's emphasis on the soul's constructive role in the origin of time goes too far. If time is, according to *Physics*, the number that is counted, not the number that counts, the soul may not 'create' or impose the temporal structure but merely find or discover it in nature. It would still be the case that time cannot exist without soul, but the latter's role may be more passive than active, more perceptive than creative. Time, in this interpretation, cannot exist *as* time without soul because there is no possible account of time in which it does not involve a subject with an awareness of time.

This awareness of time is, for Aristotle, more or less tantamount to the ability to count. In view of later developments, this may be the single most remarkable deficiency in Aristotle's theory. Is human temporality really only the capacity to measure years, and days, and hours? There is little here of the human experience of time, of memories and expectations, of hopes and disappointments, of historical experience and future projects. Perhaps Aristotle did not think these were suitable questions for the *Physics*; it is remarkable that Paul Ricoeur in his influential *Time and Narrative* draws on Aristotle's *Poetics*, not the treatise on time in *Physics*.[39] Be this as it may, it matters for the subsequent history that Aristotle holds out the significance of experiential time without, however, filling this concept beyond the rudimentary idea that the mind alone is capable of counting moments.

There is another line of questioning to which the present exposition of Aristotle's account of time and soul may give rise. Is it not the case, it may be asked, that Aristotle's *Physics* is far from being the kind of empirical philosophy of nature as it has here been presented? Does not Aristotle insist that the natural world is a hierarchical order of beings whose ultimate foundation is the perfection of the unmoved mover?[40] Moreover, does not Aristotle associate this perfect being with mind, and does he not, in *Metaphysics*, also introduce ensouled beings in the sphere of the fixed stars?[41] Finally, do we not know from the *De anima* that for Aristotle the human soul, too, is somehow connected with the perfect, eternal mind?[42]

The answer to all these questions, of course, must be given in the affirmative. As we shall see, major readers of the Stagirite in late antiquity concluded, similar to Coope, that Aristotle could not have envisaged a temporal world or

---

39 Ricoeur 1983, 66–104. Cf. further Goldschmidt 1982 and the studies collected in Balaudé 2005.
40 Aristotle, *Physics* VIII 5–6.
41 Aristotle, *Metaphysics* Λ 8.
42 Aristotle, *De anima* Γ 5.

even a changing natural world without souls or indeed an intellect because he tells us that the physical world necessarily rests on their perfection.

The question is how far this line of argument takes us in the interpretation of the present passage. I think it is entirely legitimate to point out that Aristotle clearly did not think time would ever exist – or has existed – without soul simply because he had reasons to believe that no world could exist without ensouled beings. In fact, not only Aristotle himself, his original audience too, would naturally have accepted the idea that time did not exist without soul as factually uncontroversial.

At the same time, care is always warranted in introducing contextual information into the exegesis of a particular text. *Prima facie*, Aristotle's aporia seems to be the consequence of his earlier definition of time as 'a number of change in respect of the before and after'. In this earlier discussion, however, Aristotle's references are all to human subjects and to human souls. There simply is no indication that in this connection he implied any far-reaching metaphysical assumptions about non-human souls or their role in the constitution of time.

Particular caution, furthermore, is warranted against any reading that would bring Aristotle's theory once again close to the Platonic notion of time as derived from eternity as it is clear that the entire thrust of his treatise is directed against this assumption. Time is ineluctably part of the changeable physical world and needs to be understood as such and on its own terms. Whatever contribution the human mind makes to its discovery or even its constitution – and whatever metaphysical principles may be involved in this operation – must be interpreted on the basis of this primary insight.

***

It is evident, then, that Aristotle's argument about the relationship of time and soul poses severe difficulties to any reader, and there is no indication that attempts to interpret it have become less controversial over time. No controversy should, however, exist regarding the significance of the problem raised by the Stagirite. Ultimately, the question addresses the relationship of physical, cosmic, or objective time on the one hand and the role of the human soul or mind in our experience of time on the other. While Aristotle based his philosophical theory of time on physical reality (the succession of 'before and after' inherent in the cosmos insofar as natural things are continually moving and changing) this very approach leads him to recognise the problem of experiential time.

Leaving behind for a moment the specifically Aristotelian intellectual framework within which this *aporia* is formulated, it is, I think, immediately clear that Aristotle by no means made a 'silly mistake', regardless of the plausibility of his conclusions. Rather, he points to a fundamental problem inherent in any theory of time that has lost none of its significance: How can we understand the ontological status of time if we accept on the one hand that time obviously exists independently of the awareness of it by any given individual – put simply, it does not stop while we sleep – while recognising on the other hand that it necessarily exists in and for a subject?

Ancient readers disagreed on the interpretation of Aristotle's view on time no less than his modern students do. It will be the task of subsequent chapters to chart in outline the history of these interpretations throughout the centuries that followed. Chapter two will investigate the discussion of Aristotle's view of time and soul among Peripatetic philosophers. Chapter three will turn to their Neoplatonic successors between the third and the sixth centuries of the common era. Chapter four will then deal with some Christian thinkers of that period. From this overview will emerge a remarkable variety of interpretations, but it will also become clear how each one of them engendered their own difficulties in trying to relate time and soul.

2 Time and Soul in the Peripatetic Tradition

Time without soul: Boethus of Sidon

To the best of our knowledge, the debate about Aristotle's *aporia* began with a man called Boethus of Sidon.¹ For a long time, Boethus was hardly studied. The first edition of the scant remains of his writings was only published in 2020.² Yet Boethus was clearly one of the most important philosophical thinkers of the first century BCE.³ Unfortunately, we know practically nothing about his life. His name suggests that he hailed from Sidon in today's Lebanon, but even his rough assignment to the latter half of the century and possibly the early first century CE is based on circumstantial reasoning.⁴ It seems clear that Boethus belonged to the second generation of scholars who contributed to a rapid and highly successful renewal of philosophy in the Aristotelian tradition.

Boethus's teacher, Andronicus of Rhodes, was the originator of this revival.⁵ He is associated with a new edition of Aristotle's works which provided a novel basis for scholarly interest in and the interpretation of the Stagirite. Boethus seems to have followed Andronicus as head of the Aristotelian school in Athens, the *Peripatos*. Together with Andronicus, it was Boethus who gave to ancient philosophy an unprecedented new direction by developing the practice of philosophy through the interpretation of classical texts. No philosophical school had previously entertained this idea which was to loom large over the subsequent history of philosophy. Throughout antiquity, the works of Aristotle remained the principal object of detailed, philosophical study⁶ even when, from the third century onwards, the commentators were mostly Neoplatonists.

There is little doubt that this development had its own internal rationality. Among the many texts Aristotle had produced during his lifetime, the so-called exoteric ones, which he intended and prepared by himself for publication, are

---

1 On Boethus see: Moraux 1973–2001, vol. 1, 143–79; Reinhardt 2007; Rashed 2013; Griffin 2015, 177–99.
2 Chiaradonna/Rashed 2020.
3 Rashed 2013, 53.
4 Griffin 2015, 182.
5 Griffin 2015, 21–77. On the relation of Andronicus and Boethus also Reinhardt 2007.
6 In fact, from the very beginning interest in *commenting* on Aristotle's works was not limited to Peripatetics. Cf. Chiaradonna 2013, 44: 'During the second half of the [first] century [BCE], the approach to Aristotle had changed substantially even among philosophers […], who definitely did not identify themselves as Peripatetic.'

OpenAccess. © 2022 Johannes Zachhuber, 2022, published by De Gruyter. This work is licensed under the Creative Commons Attribution-NonCommercial-NoDerivatives 4.0 International License.
https://doi.org/10.1515/978-3-11-069275-4-004

now almost completely lost.⁷ What we know today as the works of the Stagirite were, by contrast, notes he produced as part of his lecturing activity in the Lyceum. These texts often aimed at a kind of didactic systematicity, with introductions explaining the topic of a particular course, the presentation and discussion of the works of predecessors, definitions, thesis statements, and summaries of the argumentation up to a particular point. Due simply to these literary elements, Aristotle's works were more conducive to scholastic interpretations than the genres preferred by some of his competitors, notably the dialogues written by his teacher, Plato. At the same time, Aristotle's language in the extant texts is unpolished, dense and occasionally at the limits of intelligibility which, in turn, made them seem in need of commentary for their elucidation.

A key decision taken by Andronicus or, more likely, even before him was an arrangement of Aristotle's works in the order in which they ought to be read.⁸ As part of this overall decision, the writing known to us as the *Categories* came to stand at the beginning of the logical works and thus at the beginning of the corpus as a whole. As a result, the *Categories* took on a unique significance as a supposedly introductory text into the philosophy of Aristotle and, eventually, into philosophy as a whole. It didn't lose this significance for almost 1,500 years.

It is unlikely that the *Categories* were ever intended for this role although it is impossible to be entirely sure about its original place among the works of Aristotle. It lacks an introduction and thus any explanation of the author's intention in writing the brief treatise.⁹ It is doubtful that it was meant as a work of logic and, in any event, it contains many statements of an ontological character. From these statements, although they are not brought into the kind of systematic structure to be found in the central books of the *Metaphysics*, a view of reality emerges that in crucial ways is in tension with that to be found in other influential works by the Stagirite, notably the *Physics* and the *Metaphysics*.¹⁰

It is therefore important for understanding Boethus' particular take on Aristotle's theory of time and his statements on time and soul that his approach to Aristotle was largely determined by the *Categories*.¹¹ In fact, it now seems likely that the explicit comments from him about the *aporia* from Book IV of the *Physics* may have been located in a full commentary of the *Categories* which we know he composed. This, in any event, is the place assigned to them in the recent ed-

---

7 Sharples 2007.
8 The historical details of this development are somewhat murky and have been hotly debated in specialist scholarship. Cf. Sharples 2008; Chiaradonna 2013 44–6.
9 Frede 1987a.
10 Frede 1987b.
11 Rashed 2013, 53.

ition of his extant fragments and testimonia.[12] Even though it may be impossible to ascertain with final certitude whether this editorial decision is justified, there is little reason to contest its underlying interpretative insight, namely, that Boethus' Aristotelianism was crucially informed by his reading of the *Categories*.

Towards the beginning of this writing, Aristotle divided all beings based on whether or not they are 'said of a subject' and whether or not they are 'in a subject'.[13] Only those beings that are neither in a subject nor said of a subject are ontologically foundational. These beings are called primary substances and from the examples Aristotle offers it is clear that they are concrete individuals, such as 'an individual human being or a horse'.

Boethus was one of the first or the first to note the discrepancy between this theory of being and the one espoused in the central books of *Metaphysics* where Aristotle introduced three kinds of substances, matter, form, and the composite of both suggesting that of those three it was form that was most basic.[14] Faced with this conflicting textual tradition, Boethus characteristically opted for the scheme found in *Categories* from which he developed with remarkable rigour a form of Aristotelianism for which only empirical objects were ontologically foundational. Boethus considered forms as accidents inhering in matter. It therefore was ultimately matter which lay at the foundation of the world.[15]

This has wide-ranging consequences for his overall interpretation of the Aristotelian corpus. Marwan Rashed is surely correct to characterise this interpretation by ascribing to Boethus the tendency to remove the ontological 'grey zone' typical of many of Aristotle's writings.[16] What he means by that can be seen from the account given in the previous chapter. The reader of Aristotle's treatise on time is faced with the tensional unity of a physical theory of time in which time is tied to movement and change, and a more mentalist theory expressed in the definition of time as a number. Expressed in terms of school affiliations, the former of those is the 'anti-Platonic' Aristotle whereas the latter seems more willing to compromise in this regard. The claim that time could not exist without soul is arguably one of the strongest manifestations of the latter tendency, certainly within the treatise on time.

---

[12] Chiaradonna/Rashed 2020, 61–5 (fr. 37–8); 231–4. Moraux assumed that Boethus had written either 'einen regelrechten Kommentar [i.e. on the *Physics*] oder […] ein kürzeres, besonderen Teilen der Physik gewidmetes Werk' (1973–2001, vol. 1, 170).
[13] Aristotle, *Categories* 2 (1a20–1b9).
[14] Aristotle, *Metaphysics* Z 3. Cf. Griffin, 178–9.
[15] Chiaradonna/Rashed 2020, 36–7 (fr. 18); Rashed 2013, 54–5.
[16] Rashed 2011, 69.

Boethus' response to the problem indicates that he recognised it for the challenge to his Aristotelianism that it was.[17] For his engagement with the *aporia* of *Physics* IV 14, we have two fragments. They are brief and leave many important questions open. Nevertheless, it seems that his critique was fairly straightforward. Both Themistius and Simplicius report a fragment, in which Boethus rejects the proposition that time cannot exist without soul in the following words:

> Nothing prevents that something countable exists without someone counting as much as the perceptible exists without someone perceiving.[18]

Although Boethus in this fragment does not explicitly refer to either time or soul, there is no doubt that it is a comment on Aristotle's *aporia*, specifically the claim that 'if it is impossible for there to be something to do the counting, it is impossible also that anything should be countable.'[19] According to Boethus, the conclusion does not follow. After all, he seems to imply, five apples are five apples regardless of the existence of someone counting them.

The force of his argument is strengthened by an analogy. It is, he suggests, as absurd to deny that something countable exists without someone to count, as it would be to deny that perceptibles exist without perception. That perceptible things can exist without anyone perceiving them was indeed a claim Aristotle made on several occasions. In *Metaphysics* Γ, for example, he declares it impossible that 'the subjects (*hupokeimena*) which cause the perception should not exist even without perception'.[20] Boethus thus could cite Aristotelian precedent for his claim that no soul was needed in order for time to exist.

Was this meant as an explicit criticism of Aristotle himself? I do not think the answer to this question is self-evident. There is good reason to believe that Boethus was without scruples when it came to a critical assessment of the founder of the school. As we have seen, he was conscious of the tension between the ontology of *Categories* and that of the central books of *Metaphysics* in view of which he made clear his preference for the former over the latter. In the case of the *aporia*, however, we need to remember that Aristotle had presented a puzzle. Clearly, Boethus felt the answer to the question of whether time could exist

---

17 For an analysis of Boethus' interpretation of Aristotle's *aporia* see Jeck 1994, 14–6.
18 Chiaradonna/Rashed 2020, 63 (fr. 37b): μηδὲν κωλύειν τὸ ἀριθμητὸν ὥσπερ καὶ δίχα τοῦ ἀριθμοῦντος, ὥσπερ καὶ τὸ αἰσθητὸν δίχα τοῦ αἰσθανομένου.
19 Aristotle, *Physics* IV 14 (223a22–3): ἀδυνάτου γὰρ ὄντος εἶναι τοῦ ἀριθμήσοντος ἀδύνατον καὶ ἀριθμητόν τι εἶναι.
20 Aristotle, *Metaphysics* Γ 5 (1010b, 34–5): τὸ δὲ τὰ ὑποκείμενα μὴ εἶναι, ἃ ποιεῖ τὴν αἴσθησιν, καὶ ἄνευ αἰσθήσεως, ἀδύνατον.

without soul had to be given in the affirmative, but it is entirely possible that, like other readers of the Stagirite, he believed that it was Aristotle himself who wanted this conclusion to be drawn.

The same explanation might, however, become more difficult depending on how we understand the second fragment which is transmitted in the same connection. Themistius cites Boethus as saying that 'no measure comes about naturally, but both measuring and counting are in fact our activity.'[21]

Paul Moraux, in his classic study of the Aristotelian tradition, found here an explicit attack on Aristotle's definition of time. According to him, it was 'probable' that Boethus here 'wanted to distance himself from the Aristotelian definition of time and show that this kind of time, when understood as measure, loses any physical reality and is reduced to a thought in the human soul.'[22]

Based on the wording of the fragment, this is a possible interpretation. In fact, Themistius, our fourth-century source for the text, seems to have taken Boethus to mean something along those lines as he glosses his citation with the comment that Aristotle 'seems to grant' that time is 'a conception of our soul and [does] not have a nature of its own.'[23] The question is how likely it is that Boethus would have fundamentally rejected Aristotle's definition. For once, there is no indication in either Themistius or Simplicius that this fragment came from a discussion of the part of *Physics* IV in which Aristotle had put forth his definition. Instead, it appears in the context of their discussion of *Physics* IV 14.

Moreover, had Boethus fundamentally rejected the definition of time as number as unduly subjective, there would have been no reason for him *also* to engage with the problem of whether something countable could exist without someone counting, i.e. the specific problem of the *aporia*. The puzzle would not be a puzzle if the definition of time was detached from its character as number in the first place. It is, therefore, far more likely that Boethus' comment about 'measuring and counting' as 'our activity' is his own attempt to determine the meaning of Aristotle's definition rather than its blunt rejection.

In order to see how this is possible, Chiaradonna and Rashed in their edition of Boethus' fragments have proposed to restrict the literal citation to the latter half of Themistius' sentence making Boethus merely say that 'measuring and counting are in fact our activity'. This, they explain would permit finding here

---

21 Chiaradonna/Rashed 2020, 63 (fr. 38a): ὥσπερ γάρ φησι Βόηθος, οὐδὲν μέτρον ὑπὸ τῆς φύσεως γίνεται, ἀλλ' ἡμέτερον ἤδη καὶ τὸ μετρεῖν καὶ τὸ ἀριθμεῖν ἔργον ἐστίν'.
22 Moraux 1973–2001, vol. 1, 171.
23 Chiaradonna/Rashed 2020, 63 (fr. 38a): ἔννοιαν εἶναι τῆς ἡμετέρας ψυχῆς τὸν χρόνον φύσιν δὲ οἰκείαν μὴ ἔχειν, ὥσπερ ἔοικεν ἐνδώσειν Ἀριστοτέλης.

a subtle distinction between the act of *measuring* and of *counting* on the one hand and the measure and the number on the other. They suggest that Boethus assigns the former to the category of action whereas the latter belong to that of quantity.[24]

While accepting the editors' textual reconstruction of the fragment, one could alternatively find in Boethus' wording a reference to Aristotle's famous but somewhat obscure distinction between number as 'counted and countable' and number as 'that by which we count'.[25] In other words, Boethus' use of 'measuring' and 'counting' in the present place might be a reminder that, according to Aristotle himself, time was number in a specific sense and that it was this specific sense which saved it from being simply 'our own activity'. If so, Boethus would have subtly used Aristotle's own determination of time as the number that is counted to argue that time cannot be dependent on the existence of soul.

There is no doubt that much here must remain speculative. Yet the broader picture is clearer than one might think based on the complications engendered by the interpretation of Boethus' extant comments on the *aporia* from *Physics* IV 14. Boethus wanted nothing to do with the idea that soul played an essential role in the existence of time. Time, rather, is a continuous quantity, as Aristotle had called it in the *Categories* and as Boethus apparently went to great lengths to affirm against the earlier opposition of his own teacher, Andronicus.[26] To the extent that time is counted, this activity is merely the recognition of a reality that fundamentally exists independently of any human perception of it, in the same way any other aspect of physical reality exists in principle independently of human (or indeed of any) perception.

***

Up to this point, the question has not been raised what soul Boethus may have thought was at issue in Aristotle's *aporia*. I have cautioned above against an overly cosmological interpretation of Aristotle's own words, but it is plausible that Hellenistic readers, when pondering the weight of the puzzle posed in *Physics* IV, would have asked themselves whether the problem did not extend beyond the purely psychological level. After all, it is hard to accept that anyone would believe the existence of time could depend on the soul (or the mind) of an indi-

---

24 Ibid., 232.
25 Aristotle, *Physics* IV 11 (219b6–8).
26 Chiaradonna/Rashed 2020, 227–8.

vidual person given that time clearly existed before that person came into the world and will continue after their death. Insofar as time evidently existed on a cosmic scale, its dependence on soul would, arguably, be in the final instance a dependence on a cosmic soul.

We know that this conclusion was drawn by the second-century Peripatetic philosopher, Alexander of Aphrodisias, whose treatment of Aristotle's *aporia* will be analysed in the next section. As for Boethus, there is no evidence that he ever discussed the cosmic soul let alone its relationship with time. And yet it is not far-fetched to speculate that he saw the need to speak up against the notion that time could not exist without soul because he knew that such a cosmic soul was accepted by Platonists and Stoics. In other words, those rival accounts of nature would have generated the need for Boethus to be so categorical with regard to the relationship of time and soul.

The same conclusion was reached by Chiaradonna and Rashed who think (speculatively) that a section in Themistius' *Paraphrase of Aristotle's Physics* may be based on Boethus. They write accordingly that Boethus 'excluded the soul from the constitution of time in a twofold manner [...,] by admitting the existence of something countable without someone who counts' and by explaining time at the cosmic level 'not through the presence of a soul in the astral spheres, but through the mechanical regularity of the heavenly movement'.[27] Note however that even the passage in Themistius putatively assigned here to Boethus does not refer to the cosmic soul. We therefore have to accept that the evidence that Boethus' sharp categorical rejection of time's dependence on soul is at best indirectly connected with the issue of a cosmic soul.

In sum, Boethus rejected the notion that time depends for its existence on the soul. Time, for him, was an objective reality existing in nature independently of its psychological or mental identification and measurement. This view, it appears, was part of a broader programme of an Aristotelianism as a philosophy of natural or physical being developed largely from Boethus' interpretation of the *Categories*. This version of Aristotelianism welcomed sharp distinctions especially from Stoicism and Platonism. It would therefore have suited a situation in which the Peripatetic school sought to re-establish itself in relation to a plurality of institutional rivals. At the same time, Boethus was hardly an Aristotelian 'fundamentalist'. On the contrary, he seems to have been perfectly capable of critiquing individual expressions and ideas found in the master's works.

When we come to the end of the second century CE, we encounter a very different situation. On the one hand, the traditional competition between schools is

---

27 Ibid., 234. Cf. Themistius, *In Aristotelis physica paraphrasis* (163, 7–18 Schenkl).

receding which results in a growing tendency to find agreements between traditional positions rather than to emphasise their differences. As we shall see, this development led to a novel appreciation of the nuances in Aristotle's own view. Although initially advanced within the Peripatos, this novel interpretation ultimately paved the way for the Neoplatonic appropriation of Aristotelian philosophy as fundamentally compatible with Platonism.

At the same time, the authoritative status of the Aristotelian text grew and the willingness to criticise him abated. Commentators were increasingly keen to explain difficulties, tensions, and even contradictions through subtle interpretative moves or by introducing distinctions that could explain why the Stagirite had expressed himself in this way rather than that. Both these tendencies, as we shall see, are at play in the further interpretation of the *aporia* of *Physics* IV 14.

Alexander of Aphrodisias: commentator and philosopher

Up until this point, the focus of this account has been almost exclusively on the problem of time. Both in Aristotle and in Boethus, it seemed that the problem of whether time could exist without soul was primarily or exclusively a problem of the nature of time. By contrast, the question of the nature of soul has found little attention so far. Yet it was inevitable that, once the puzzle presented by the Stagirite in *Physics* IV was more thoroughly investigated, this question would gain an increasingly central significance. After all, how could one adjudicate on the inter-dependency of time and soul without a clear understanding of both realities?

While it is possible that this question was broached by Boethus already, the first clear evidence we possess for its discussion stems from the work of Alexander of Aphrodisias. Alexander, about whose life we once again know next to nothing, was the towering figure of Peripatetic philosophy in the imperial era.[28] From the dedication of one of his works to the emperors Septimus Severus and Caracalla, whose co-reign lasted from 198 to 209 CE, we can assign his activity to the turn of the third century and thus at least 200 years after Boethus.[29] We know little about the intervening period of Aristotelian commentary, and nothing has come down to us that would indicate any particular interest during this considerable time span for the question of time and soul.

---

28 The most comprehensive treatments are now: Moraux 1973–2001, vol. 3 and Rashed 2007.
29 Frede 2017.

Alexander's fame in posterity is summed up in his honorific title of 'the commentator'. He was seen as the paradigmatic exegete whose line-by-line commentaries on the Stagirite's philosophical writings became authoritative sources for the Neoplatonist commentators of late antiquity, whose practice was subsequently adopted by Syriac, Arabic, and Latin philosophers as well.

By contrast, Alexander was less recognised as a philosopher in his own right.[30] For the Middle Ages, which knew his work mainly thorough Arabic intermediaries, he was the radical Aristotelian whose views spawned the heterodox Aristotelianism of the thirteenth century. It has only been the result of recent, painstaking philological and philosophical research that Alexander now appears as a major original thinker with the project of claiming for the Peripatetic tradition the *via media* between Stoicism and Platonism and thus, *nolens volens* adopting a Platonising interpretation of Aristotle's thought.[31]

The striking plausibility of this interpretation appears once we recall that one of the most celebrated (or to some notorious) aspects of the Neoplatonic commentary tradition that emerged from the third century was the fundamental harmony of Plato and Aristotle, while for the same tradition Alexander evidently was the main exegetical authority.[32] The integration of Aristotle's text into the Neoplatonic curriculum has often been explained by the institutional necessities of the philosophical schools at the time. The underlying philosophical harmonisation of the Platonic and the Aristotelian traditions rested, it is then presumed, on a brilliant but again rather pragmatic separation of their respective spheres, according to which Aristotle mainly dealt with the visible world while Plato taught about the intelligible world, the *mundus intelligibilis*.

Bringing Alexander into the picture shows the limits of this narrative and reveals that the 'harmony of Plato and Aristotle' was to an extent at least the result of serious textual study and philosophical reflection contributing to the legitimate reconciliation of the two different approaches. As we shall see, it is this moderately Platonising tendency encountered in Alexander which characterises his interpretation of Aristotle's comments on time and soul as well.

---

30 Kupreeva 2010, 211–2.
31 This, at least, is Rashed's project for which cf. Rashed 2007, 324–7 and the discussion in Kupreeva 2010.
32 Karamanolis 2006; cf. Hadot 2015, 51–3.

Alexander on Aristotle's *aporia*

Unfortunately, Alexander's *Commentary on Aristotle's Physics* does not survive in its original version. It seems clear, however, that his commentary constitutes the authoritative interpretation of Aristotle's difficult text which was subsequently accepted as valid by the major Neoplatonist commentators, Porphyry of Tyre (234?-305? CE) and by Simplicius of Cilicia (ca. 480–560) whose massive commentary we do possess. Simplicius offers extensive extracts from Alexander's work. In addition, there are Byzantine *scholia* to Alexander's commentary which help identify further parts of Simplicius' text as originating from Alexander's work.[33] A further resource for our understanding of Alexander's conception of time is a treatise *De tempore*, which is however available to us only in Arabic and Latin.[34]

Simplicius tells us that Alexander discussed Aristotle's *aporia* 'in detail' (διὰ πλειόνων) with special regard to the position he found in Boethus.[35] In fact, it is likely that the information we possess about the latter's interpretation is entirely derived from Alexander's engagement with it. Alexander fundamentally rejected Boethus' interpretation. For him, Aristotle meant to affirm that time could not exist without soul, and he was right to think so. This Alexander initially sought to establish through a careful recalibration of the argument Boethus had offered for the opposite view.[36]

Despite his critical attitude towards his predecessor, Alexander's engagement with Boethus was not polemical but written from the conviction that they shared the same philosophical outlook in principle even while disagreeing on points of detail. We have seen how Boethus' argument rested on the idea that what is counted can perfectly well exist without someone counting it. Alexander counters this by introducing a further distinction:

> It is worth investigating how sound the statement is that there is nothing enumerable if there is nothing that will enumerate. That there is nothing enumerable or enumerated *qua* enumerated if there is nothing that enumerates can be allowed, if being enumerated is essential to number. But what is enumerable itself, i.e. what is capable of being enumerated, such as men or horses, does not seem to be annihilated with the enumerator. Aris-

---

[33] Rashed 2011.
[34] Sharples 1982.
[35] Simplicius, *In Aristotelis physicorum libros commentaria* (759, 19–20 Diels).
[36] For a detailed analysis of Alexander's critique of Boethus see Rashed 2011, 69–74. Cf. also Jeck 1994, 17–25.

totle himself shows that the before and after in change, which are enumerable, can exist without soul, at least if there can be change without soul.³⁷

Alexander thus concedes to his predecessor that counted objects can exist without being counted. 'Men or horses', as he writes, will not be done away with if the person counting them is done away with. If there were previously ten horses, there will still be ten horses even when no one is there to enumerate them. Yet they will not, so to speak, be ten *as* ten. There is, Alexander suggests, a difference between what is countable and the countable *insofar as it is* countable. Being numbered belongs to the former only 'by accident' (τὸ μὲν ᾧ συμβέβηκεν ἀριθμητῷ γίνεσθαι), whereas it is the latter which irreducibly depends on the subject that counts.³⁸

Alexander seeks to substantiate this differentiation by referring to the final part of Aristotle's puzzle. After arguing that time could not exist without soul, the Stagirite seemed to concede the following qualification to that claim

> ... except that there could be that, whatever it is, by being which time is, for example, if it is possible for there to be change without soul. The before and after are in change and time is these in so far as they are countable.³⁹

Aristotle here offers a puzzle within his puzzle. Even if time cannot exist without soul, it might be that the substrate of time or that which time really is could exist without a soul. It is usually assumed that this substrate is change although Aristotle's own words seem to suggest that change is merely *one* possible candidate for that 'being which time is'.⁴⁰ Note that Aristotle does not affirm that change can exist without soul – we will see that some interpreters emphatically claim

---

37 Alexander, *In physica* IV 14, apud Simplicius, *In Aristotelis physicorum libros commentaria* (759, 21–8 Diels). ET: Urmson 1992, 173: ἄξιον γάρ, φησί, ζητῆσαι, πῶς ὑγιές ἐστι τὸ μὴ ὄντος τοῦ ἀριθμήσοντος μηδὲ ἀριθμητὸν εἶναι. τὸ μὲν γὰρ ἀριθμητὸν μὴ εἶναι μηδὲ τὸ ἀριθμούμενον καθὸ ἀριθμούμενον μὴ ὄντος τοῦ ἀριθμοῦντος, ἐχέτω λόγον, εἰ τῷ ἀριθμῷ ἐν τῷ ἀριθμεῖσθαι τὸ εἶναι· τὸ μέντοι ἀριθμητὸν αὐτὸ καὶ ὃ οἷόν τε ἀριθμηθῆναι οἷον ἄνθρωποι ἢ ἵπποι οὐ δοκεῖ τῷ ἀριθμοῦντι συναναιρεῖσθαι. τὸ γοῦν πρότερον καὶ ὕστερον ἐν κινήσει ὄντα ἀριθμητὰ δείκνυσιν αὐτὸς εἶναι δυνάμενα καὶ μὴ οὔσης ψυχῆς, εἴ γε κίνησιν οἷόν τε εἶναι μὴ οὔσης ψυχῆς.
38 Alexander, *In physica* IV 14, apud Simplicius, *In Aristotelis physicorum libros commentaria* (759, 29–30 Diels).
39 Aristotle, *Physics* IV 14 (223a27–9): ἀλλ' ἢ τοῦτο ὅ ποτε ὂν ἔστιν ὁ χρόνος, οἷον εἰ ἐνδέχεται κίνησιν εἶναι ἄνευ ψυχῆς. τὸ δὲ πρότερον καὶ ὕστερον ἐν κινήσει ἐστίν· χρόνος δὲ ταῦτ' ἐστὶν ᾗ ἀριθμητά ἐστι. ET: Coope 2005, 159.
40 E.g. Coope 2005, 160.

that he did not mean to imply that it could – but only that it could possibly do so.

Alexander in any event, seems to have read this statement as establishing a difference between time as the number of change, which as such cannot exist without soul, and change which underlies time and as such can exist without soul. Whether change *does* exist without soul is, of course, an entirely different matter.[41]

In his formal solution to the problem posed by Boethus, Alexander refers to the category of relation:

> In the case of other relatives, if, for instance, there is nobody on the right, he who was on the left, Socrates perhaps, will exist, but a person on the left will not. So, if time were enumerable as the before and after are enumerable, if there were no one enumerating there would be no time. But nothing prevents the substrate of time, which is change, from existing.[42]

Time like 'being on the left', for Alexander cannot fully and truly exist without its correlative. By contrast, one might say that nothing changes about Socrates regardless of whether anyone stands on his right or not. Likewise, Alexander seems willing to concede that a world with change occurring in the structure of 'before and after' but without someone counting its instances, the change would still be there, but it would not be time.

The bigger picture, as Rashed has proposed, is that Alexander seeks to enrich the kind of Aristotelian ontology to be found in Boethus.[43] For the latter, things either had to exist as physical reality or they did not exist at all. Alexander, by contrast, seems more willing to recognise (and accept) the existence of beings that, while having their foundation in physical reality cannot simply be identified with it.

---

[41] Ursula Coope has argued that for Aristotle ultimately neither time nor change exists without soul, but that change *could* exist without soul whereas time could not. Perhaps this was Alexander's interpretation as well. Coope 2005, 161–3.

[42] Alexander, *In physica* IV 14, *apud* Simplicius, *In Aristotelis physicorum libros commentaria* (759, 31–760, 3 Diels). ET: Urmson 1992, 173 [with changes]: καὶ γὰρ καὶ ἐπὶ τῶν ἄλλων πρός τι μὴ ὄντως εἰ τύχοι τοῦ δεξιοῦ, ὃς μὲν ἦν ἀριστερὸς ἔσται οἷον Σωκράτης, ἀριστερὸς δὲ οὔ. εἰ οὖν τὸ πρότερον καὶ ὕστερον ὡς ἀριθμητὰ ἀριθμητὸς ὁ χρόνος ἦν, μὴ ὄντος τοῦ ἀριθμήσοντος οὐκ ἂν εἴη ὁ χρόνος. τὸ μέντοι τῷ χρόνῳ ὑποκείμενον, ὅπερ ἦν ἡ κίνησις, οὐδὲν κωλύει εἶναι.

[43] Rashed 2011, 71–2: 'Pour Boéthos, le temps est soit quelque chose d'objectif – c'est-à-dire une caractéristique objective, à l'instar d'une qualité ou d'une quantité, de la chose dans un temps – soit rien du tout. Pour Alexandre, en revanche, il peut y avoir des étants dont l'être consiste dans une certaine détermination autonome, qui n'est pas le pur être-là d'une matière ou de l'accident qui lui est inhérent, mais qui est la structure d'ordre du substrat.'

Time and the cosmic soul

Alexander's engagement with Boethus can easily appear overly subtle, scholastic or even artificial. This partly results from the underlying agreement between the two authors. They cannot cite fundamental philosophical principles to settle their differences because they both share their most important philosophical assumptions. Moreover, they both seek to establish philosophical answers to complex questions through the interpretation of one and the same authoritative text, which leads to the application of increasingly sophisticated exegetical and hermeneutical tools.

Yet the scholastic garment in which this argument is clad must not obscure for us the significance of what is at stake. There is a reason why Boethus' and Alexander's viewpoints remained at the centre of the subsequent commentary tradition. Underlying their subtle differences about distinctions and interpretations is a problem that is not trivial at all: the ontological status of time and its relation to consciousness. So far, not much of this has been visible although it was evident that, against Boethus, Alexander was keen to find in Aristotle a view of time that moves it away from its physical basis by aligning it with its subjective appropriation through the rational being that experiences time.

In what appears to have been a second part of his comment on the *aporia*, however, Alexander apparently went a crucial step further, thereby making his own contribution to the history of interpretation of Aristotle's difficult text. As we shall see, this additional interpretative claim reverberated through the later tradition where unequivocally Platonic readers of Aristotle pushed it into a direction which the Peripatetic thinker could never have accepted even though he laid its foundations.

The reconstruction of this argument is complicated by the fact that it has to draw on three different sources: the Byzantine scholia of Alexander's *Commentary on the Physics*; Simplicius' *Commentary on the Physics*; and the treatise *De tempore* extant in an Arabic (and a later Latin) translation. We saw that Alexander in his initial response to Boethus read the penultimate sentence in the Aristotelian *aporia* as a factual statement affirming the existence of motion without soul even though such an interpretation is not mandated by Aristotle's rather tentative formulation: 'should there be motion without soul'. In fact, as we have already observed, there are good reasons to assume that for Aristotle motion could *in fact* never exist without a soul regardless of his views about the relationship of time and soul.[44]

---

44 Cf. again Coope 2005, 163.

It is therefore in a sense not too surprising that Alexander went on to make this exact point. In the *Scholia* his argument is presented as follows:

> In any event, if there is no soul, no movement would at all be possible. For there will not be the circular movement which comes about through <desire>,[45] by means of the mind, nor the movements of living beings. For the human being is begotten by the sun. And that waxing-and-waning and the changes are suspended from the circular movement [of the spheres] is evident.[46]

The same idea is also encountered in the *De tempore*:

> And if the soul were done away with the heavenly sphere would not be moved; and if this were not moved, all movements would be done away with, since it is the cause of all movements, and so of time.[47]

Alexander's argument probably still responds to Boethus who may have claimed that cosmic time can be fully explained by reference to the circular movement of the heavenly sphere. Be this as it may, Alexander who had initially conceded that the definition of time as number did not require the co-dependency of change and soul, now observes that the *possibility* of the existence of time without soul is in practice excluded by the principles of Aristotelian physics. For there is no motion without mind – Alexander now evidently has the unmoved mover in mind. After all, all changes and movements in the sublunar sphere – the rise and fall of the tides, the generation of human beings and the various movements of living beings – depend on the circular motion of the stars which, in its turn, is moved by its desire for the perfection of the first principle which is mind.

For the present investigation, this is a crucial moment. By means of his interpretative thesis, Alexander has established a connection between the 'counting' soul, which to the naive reader of Aristotle would appear to be the individual soul of a given human person and a cosmic soul.

With this decision, an entirely new potential of Aristotle's aporetic passage has been broached. The question is now no longer simply whether time is purely a physical reality or whether it also somehow relies on its actualisation in the consciousness of a soul or a mind (although this, admittedly, was not an entirely trivial question either). Rather, Alexander's argument opens up a novel direction for the entire debate that started from the Aristotelian passage. At issue now is

---

45 Add. Rashed from Simplicius.
46 Rashed 2011, 288 (fr. 203).
47 Sharples 1982, 64 (§ 16).

the problem of which metaphysical assumptions are necessary in order to reconcile the psychological, individual experience of time with its universal and cosmic dimension. Alexander seems to gesture at a bold solution, the existence of a universal soul or mind which both causes the motion of the heavenly sphere which is the basis of objective time, and one presumes, is connected with the mind of the individual thus synchronising the subjective experience of time with its objective reality.

That said, the question of how much of this new direction is already present in Alexander's admittedly sketchy comments, will need some further elucidation. Before entering into a closer investigation of his words, however, it is appropriate to expand somewhat on the background of what is at issue here. This necessitates taking a step back in time to Plato's theory of the world soul and its early reception.

The world soul prior to Alexander

It is arguable that the many references to a cosmic or world soul that are to be found in Western thought through the centuries can ultimately all be traced back to a few lines in Plato's dialogues, most of them to be found in his *Timaeus*.[48] In this text, a monologue more than a conversation, the eponymous speaker gives a mythical report about the creation of the world as part of which the world soul is first introduced.[49] Timaeus' whole account is geared towards the contrast between the immutable and eternal character of the forms and the transitory and overall inferior being of the sensible world. At the same time, the narrator – surely Plato's mouthpiece – is keen to emphasise the goodness and beauty of the cosmos thus created. The Craftsman (or Demiurge) who made it is described as forming the visible on the model of its perfect archetype.[50]

A key phrase through which Timaeus expresses his appreciation of the visible, created world is that it is a 'living being'.[51] As such it is 'the created image of the eternal gods' that is, it approaches perfection as far as possible. It is in line with this emphasis on the world as a living being, then, that Timaeus relates that the world was created with a soul and not just a body. In fact, the soul was

---

48 On the history of the world soul cf. Moreau 1939; Deuse 1983; Zachhuber 2004; Helmig 2020; Wilberding 2021. On the Platonic view in particular cf. Wilberding 2021a.
49 On the *Timaeus* see Cornford 1937; Wright 2000; Broadie 2011; Sattler/Mohr 2010.
50 On the interpretation of this figure as the 'mythical equivalent of *nous*', cf. Hackforth 1936; Menn 1995.
51 Plato, *Timaeus* 30b4–c1.

meant to be 'the ruler and mistress' of the body of the cosmos in line with Plato's general assumption that intelligible being ranks above the sensible.[52]

It is, then, clear that the world soul in Plato's scheme is a particularly excellent being fashioned in order to ensure that the world as a whole can partake of divine perfection as far as possible. And yet, the same logic also dictates that there is some ambivalence in the entity whose existence is thus stipulated. For while the world soul is evidently more perfect than the visible world – as the human soul is more perfect than the human body – it is also clearly *less* perfect than the intelligible realm on which it was modelled. The world soul, in Plato's logic, has to be an intermediate being and thus one step closer to the problematic realm of the sensible than its paradigm, the world of forms.

This intermediate status of the world soul is indicated where the Craftsman is said to have 'forged' into a unity divisible and indivisible Nature, Sameness, and Difference with each of the latter also mixed from the divisible and the indivisible.[53] The three main components are known to the reader of Plato's other dialogues as the highest genera of the *Sophist*;[54] the world soul is thus said to consist of everything that is. The additional reference to divisible and indivisible furthermore indicates that this mixture extends to the principal two ontological realms, the intelligible and the sensible world. The world soul thus is, we might say, a comprehensive but also tensional composite containing in itself the principles of being as well as becoming.

Where Timaeus talks about the world soul's activity, his account clearly shows the parallel between individual and cosmic souls.[55] The world soul is principally discursive concerned with the establishment of truthful knowledge. As such, it is the paradigm and source of cognition. Once again, however, it is important to note that its mode of obtaining knowledge is in line with its overall ontological status as an intermediate being. Importantly, it involves movement. In fact, the notion of the world soul as eternally self-moving and as such the origin of all movement in the world is crucial for the Platonic concept and one major point of dissent with Aristotle.

Aristotle's *On the Soul* contains a sharp attack on the cosmology of the *Timaeus* targeting principally its mythical form of presentation.[56] Elsewhere, in *On the Heavens*, he bluntly disowns the view that the cosmos 'should persist

---

52 *Ibid.* 34c5.
53 Plato, *Timaeus* 35a.
54 Cornford 1937, 61.
55 Plato, *Timaeus* 36e-37c.
56 Aristotle, *De anima* A 3 (406b26–407a1). Cf. Carter 2017.

eternally by the necessitation of a soul'.⁵⁷ There is thus no world soul in Aristotle, but one may find in the unmoved mover something of an equivalent to it. If so, however, the differences are characteristic. Whereas for Plato the world soul caused movement by being eternally self-moving, Aristotle's first cosmological principle causes all movement precisely by being itself without motion. It goes without saying, moreover, that the unmoved mover is no intermediate being, that it is not composed or mixed of anything, and its intelligence is not discursive. As the summit of perfection, it corresponds to Plato's forms or even his Form of the Good rather than the clearly less than perfect world soul.

The Stoics, by contrast, were happy to adapt the language of the *Timaeus* to their own purposes calling the world a living being controlled by a cosmic soul.⁵⁸ This adaptation, however, involved considerable conceptual changes. The cosmic soul of Stoic doctrine is simply the active principle pervading the universe and providing its internal coherence. As such, it can also be referred to as spirit (*pneuma*) or reason (*logos*).⁵⁹ The hierarchical element of Platonic doctrine is thus removed; the world soul is instead integrated into a dynamic concept of nature which is meant to explain the cosmos in its existence, its changes, and its movements immanently, that is, on its own terms.

By the time of Alexander, the world soul was frequently invoked by philosophers who drew on more than one of these sources, and it may thus be anachronistic to present these different options as if they existed as such at the end of the second century.⁶⁰ That said, it seems to me that two claims can be defended that are crucial for assessing Alexander's own intellectual contribution. First, Peripatetics generally rejected the notion of a cosmic soul. We have seen that there are (admittedly speculative) reasons to think that Boethus made a point of explaining the celestial movements without the need of a soul. As for the Peripatetic tradition between him and Alexander, this is so obscure that it would, admittedly, be difficult to be too categorical with any particular doctrinal claim, but there certainly is no indication that any of these thinkers adopted such a view or even commented on this question.

The second claim I would propose is that, despite its use in various contexts across half a millennium, there is no sign that prior to Alexander the world soul was ever connected specifically with time. As this claim arguably goes to the

---

57 Aristotle, *De caelo* B 1 (284a27–33). Cf. Johansen 2009.
58 Salles 2021.
59 Salles 2021, 45–6.
60 Cf. the account of the world soul in Atticus, a rough contemporary of Alexander's, which combines Platonic and Stoic elements. Atticus, *fr.* 8. On Atticus more generally see Dillon 1996, 247–257; Moreschini 1987. Cf. Köckert 2009, 74–8.

heart of the present argument, it will be necessary to dwell on this point a little longer. In the *Timaeus*, the creation of time is reported right after the creation of the world soul.[61] One might therefore think there is a connection between the two. And indeed, there are formulations that could invite such a conclusion notably the description of time as an 'everlasting likeness [to eternity] moving according to number'.[62] Overall the connection of time with movement, primarily the movement of the celestial sphere seems to suggest a relationship with the world soul which, as we have seen, was also described as eternally moving. In the *Laws*, Plato calls it the source of all movement for that reason.[63]

And yet there can be no doubt that in the logic of the *Timaeus* at least the two creative acts are clearly distinct and not related, at least not directly. Both, world soul and time are created by the Craftsman, but the latter is only added in connection with the creation of the heavenly bodies without which it cannot exist. Crawford correctly comments on the transition by saying 'we turn now from the spiritual motions of the World-Soul [...] to the physical motions of perceptible bodies in the Heaven'.[64] Time, moreover, seems to be not clearly distinguished from these movements in the *Timaeus*. As we have seen, Aristotle pitched his definition of time as number of change against the view that it was itself motion. The Stoics too, for whom time was simply the 'interval' (*diastema*), an entity whose ontological status could, notoriously, only be described as a something (*ti*), did not link it directly with the cosmic soul.[65]

It is, then, arguable that by the time of Alexander the tradition of the cosmic soul was (1) considered alien to Peripatetic philosophy and (2) not identified as the originator of time. On both counts, Alexander seems to have innovated, and the reason for this innovation, it seems, was his *exegetical* need to defend Aristotle's claim that time could not exist without soul. It is now time to consider more closely how he advanced this claim and what, precisely, it entailed for him.

---

61 Plato, *Timaeus* 37c-38c.
62 *Ibid.* 37d6–7.
63 Plato, *Laws* X, 896 a
64 Cornford 1937, 97.
65 On the Stoic theory of time cf. Goldschmidt 1953; Rist 1969, ch. 9; Tzamalikos 1991.

Alexander's contribution to the discussion about time and soul

When Alexander's utterances on time and soul are read against the conceptual backdrop that has just been sketched, a number of observations can at once be made.

First of all, the fundamentally Aristotelian character of his argument is apparent from his reference to mind and desire in connection with the heavenly movement.[66] This of course is abbreviated, but it clearly evokes the notion that the unmoved mover moves as the object of thought and desire.[67] Note that the argument that no movement, and thus presumably no time, would be possible without the unmoved mover (who can also be described as mind[68]) is impeccably Peripatetic and should not face objections from within a philosophy based on the authority of the Aristotelian corpus.

Yet the claim that all cosmic movement depends on the unmoved mover does not, in itself, apply to the Aristotelian *aporia* which posits that time cannot exist without soul and presents the case, as we have seen, that this is because time is number, and number needs someone to count. It is in this regard that Alexander makes his bold move by transitioning from mind to soul as if taking for granted that the two terms are interchangeable while arguably implying that, furthermore, there is a relationship between the human (rational) mind and the cosmic soul or mind. How can we understand Alexander's reasoning in connecting these seemingly disparate threads?

I take it that he finds justification for connecting soul and mind in Aristotle's own gloss specifying that the counting soul is intellect ('if nothing else has the nature to count than soul [and in the soul, the intellect]'[69]). Alexander's case then might have been that Aristotle could, instead of asking whether time can exist without soul, have asked instead right from the outset whether time could exist without mind or intellect.

The problem with this interpretation is that Alexander does not say any such thing but instead argues that without *soul* there would be no movement of the heavenly sphere. This wording is not only found in the *De tempore*, where we rely on an Arabic translation from the Greek, but equally in the scholia to his *Commentary* and in Simplicius. It must therefore be assumed that it was in Alexander's original text as well. This choice of phrase seems to suggest that

---

66 Rashed 2011 288 (fr. 203).
67 Aristotle, *Metaphysics* Λ 7 (1072a26–7).
68 Aristotle, *Metaphysics* Λ 7 (1072b18–24).
69 Aristotle, *Physics* IV 14 (223a25–6).

Alexander fundamentally had no problem aligning the notions of soul (that is, rational soul) and mind. This may seem like a small terminological shift, but it has far-reaching consequences. As I observed earlier, Aristotle rejected the idea of a world soul while introducing the unmoved mover as an alternative concept. But if the latter cannot only be called mind but also (without apparent differentiation) soul, this would indicate a considerable alignment of the two concepts.

Alexander, then, seems to think of the unmoved mover here as a kind of world soul although he retains the Aristotelian notion that it causes the circular movement of the heavens as the object of desire and thought, not as self-moving. Moreover, he also seems to stipulate a link between this soul and the human soul. This link admittedly is not entirely easy to identify because Alexander does not make it explicit in the text we possess. What can we make out about his line of thought? As it is, we seem to have two separate arguments deriving from Aristotle's *aporia*. On the one hand, Alexander justified the statement that soul was needed to count time as number on the grounds that the countable *qua* countable needed someone to count, while on the other, he clarifies Aristotle's reference to the possibility that change could exist without soul by reference to the cosmic soul which causes the movement of the celestial sphere and thus all other change as well.

At one level, the two arguments are clearly separate. Alexander does *not* say that the soul that counts must be a cosmic entity, nor does he say or even imply that the world soul is related to time insofar as it *is number*. And yet it is hard to accept that he believed Aristotle to speak of two different souls within the same paragraph or that he himself would have referred to soul twice in the same breath without thinking that the two are ultimately identical. In other words, Alexander would have understood Aristotle's *aporia* as a two-step argument which initially simply relied on the *formal* question of whether number can exist without someone counting to proceed to a metaphysical claim according to which change and time are dependent on soul in their existence and thus, I would assume, *a fortiori*, also on being counted. Although Alexander does not, then, say it explicitly in the text we possess, I find it hard to believe that he did *not* think that it is ultimately the cosmic soul that established time as number by counting it.

It is interesting in this connection that Alexander cites Aristotle's claim that 'man is begotten by man and by the sun as well'[70] as apparently one argument in support of his overall claim. This rather obscure line from Book II of the *Physics*

---

70 Aristotle, Physics II (194b13): ἄνθρωπος γὰρ ἄνθρωπον γεννᾷ καὶ ἥλιος.

was to take on considerable relevance in connection with another influential attempt to introduce the world soul into Aristotelian cosmology.⁷¹ This attempt is first attested in Themistius, a fourth-century rhetorician in Constantinople who wrote paraphrases of Aristotle's works. These works were, in reality, brief commentaries rather than mere regurgitations of Aristotle's arguments as their title might suggest. Among Themistius' works is a *Paraphrase of Aristotle's Metaphysics Λ*, a text which is not extant in Greek but only in Arabic fragments and a full Hebrew version translated from the Arabic.

In his treatment of *Metaphysics Λ* 3, Themistius criticises Aristotle's categorical rejection of Platonic forms on the grounds that the purely horizontal causation on which Aristotle's account seems to rely was insufficient to explain the world as it is.⁷² In support of this charge, Themistius cites the case of spontaneous generation, the (alleged) production of animals not through the normal process of begetting but from bodies of a different kind.⁷³ According to Themistius, this includes hornets that come into existence from the bodies of dead horses and bees from dead cattle; frogs, he claims, are generated from putrescence and mosquitoes from wine that has gone bad. These examples, which Themistius evidently takes as universally accepted instances of generation, were evidence that Aristotle's formula 'a man begets a man' could alone not explain life in its entirety. There was needed a cosmic, vertical force as well, most obviously where living beings are born without a parent but also more generally. In fact, such an additional cause, Themistius urged, was acknowledged by Aristotle himself where he listed, elsewhere in the same book, 'the father and [...] the sun and the inclined sphere' among the causes of a human person.⁷⁴

According to Themistius, this reference proves that the principles (*logoi*) of human generation

> [...] have been inspired by a cause nobler, more venerable and higher in rank than it [sc. nature], namely the soul that is in the earth which Plato had thought had been created by the secondary gods, and Aristotle had thought had been created by the sun and the inclined sphere.⁷⁵

---

71 For what follows cf. Zachhuber 2020.
72 Aristotle, *Metaphysics Λ* 3 (1070a27–30). Themistius, *In Aristotelis metaphysicorum librum Λ paraphrasis* (א, 2-ח, 28). ET: Meyrav 2020, 35–7. For a full discussion of Themistius' argument cf. Meyrav 2017.
73 For the history of this idea cf. now Lehoux 2017.
74 Aristotle, *Metaphysics Λ* 12 (1071a15–6).
75 Meyrav 2020, 36.

Quite what Themistius means here by the 'soul that is in the earth', what the reference to the 'secondary gods' of the *Timaeus* signifies or why any of this helps him with his criticism of Aristotle, is hard to understand.⁷⁶ Yet it is arguable that
(1) The entity he has in view is the ultimate 'vertical' cause Themistius believes Aristotle needed to acknowledge in addition to the 'horizontal' logic contained in his slogan that 'a man begets a man';
(2) He believes this entity is a soul that is also in view where Aristotle refers to the 'sun and its oblique course' in *Metaphysics* Λ 5;
(3) There is, on this point a rapprochement between Aristotle's cosmology and Plato's *Timaeus*.

It is, then, interesting that in another passage Themistius clearly referred to the world soul to account for spontaneous generation:

> That it is reasonable for the soul of the universe to irradiate either soul or ensoulment to bodies by being a vital force extended through the universe would seem to be above all evident in spontaneously generated animals, which right [at birth] breathe, live and are self-moved through their particular bodily temperament, as is reported of mice in Egypt, and as do worms, gnats and many similar animal species known to us.⁷⁷

Here, Themistius rather straightforwardly asserts that spontaneous generation provides evidence for the presence of a universal soul across the whole cosmos. While there is, admittedly, some risk in using this text to clarify the passage from the *Paraphrase on Metaphysics*, I would tentatively conclude that the best overall explanation is that Themistius testifies to a view according to which Aristotle's reference to the 'sun' in connection with human generation should be taken to justify a more 'Platonising' interpretation of the Stagirite's cosmology involving a world soul responsible for universal ensoulment. Themistius' recent editor, Yoav Meyrav, called this 'a rather irresponsible syncretism',⁷⁸ but it is notable that Themistius' later Arabic readers, notably Ibn Rushd (Averroes) for whom this passage was of great importance, certainly understood him along the lines I have just proposed.⁷⁹

In the present context, however, the problem of how to interpret Themistius is less important than the question of his possible sources. Could one of them have been Alexander? Such a possibility must come with clear caveats to obtain

---

76 Cf. Zachhuber 2020, 343.
77 Themistius, *In libros de anima paraphrasis* (26, 25–30 Heinze). ET: Todd 1996, 42–3.
78 Meyrav 2017, 206, n. 28.
79 Zachhuber 2020, 344–6.

any plausibility. Alexander would not, obviously, have launched the kind of attack on Aristotle that we encounter in Themistius. Nor would he have speculated about Plato's soul of the earth about which we hear, it seems, for the first time in Plotinus.[80]

On the other hand, it does not take much to assign to Alexander the interpretation of Aristotle that is evidently underlying Themistius' own argument. According to this interpretation, which is more presupposed than explicated by the fourth-century author, Aristotle's reference to the sun in addition to the parent as a cause of the individual's generation indicates that changes in the sublunar world are directly dependent on supralunar beings and, more specifically, on a cosmic soul.

That this was Alexander's position seems hardly doubtful in view of his comment on the *aporia* of *Physics* IV 14 as well as other relevant texts as shown by Rashed.[81] Where Themistius may help, however, is in the clarification of the kind of connection that exists between the cosmic soul and the individual human being. If we may impute to Alexander a view along the lines of Themistius' formulation that 'it is reasonable for the soul of the universe to irradiate either soul or ensoulment to bodies',[82] this could explain how Alexander believed the stipulation of a cosmic soul could explain *both* the existence of change *and* the existence of a subject that could count time.

How plausible such a reconstruction is must depend largely on the implications of the reference to the line 'man begets man and so does the sun'. According to Rashed's full presentation of Alexander's philosophy, this Aristotelian statement was central to the cosmology of the philosopher from Aphrodisias.[83] As Rashed points out

> The whole originality of the position of the Exegete [i.e. Alexander] was his insistence in his interpretation of this dictum on the role of the *sun* understood as the representative of the continuity of the heavenly movement and thus as the guarantee for the perpetuity of the succession of earthly generations.[84]

If this is accepted, it does not seem outlandish to assume that Themistius drew on Alexander insofar as he employed an interpretation of the Stagirite along those lines. This interpretation, then, would permit us to conclude that Alexand-

---

[80] Plotinus, *Ennead* IV 4; cf. Meyrav 2017, 205, n. 26.
[81] Rashed 2007, 278–85.
[82] Todd 1996, 42.
[83] Rashed 2007, 285.
[84] *Ibid.*

er's brief reference to the 'sun' in his interpretation of Aristotle's *aporia* was meant to invoke a chain of assumptions which could explain the link between cosmic and subjective time on an Aristotelian basis. The soul which counts time would thus identify time as a real dimension of the physical universe that existed as a consequence of change. Change, however, was ultimately caused by a cosmic soul which also bore direct responsibility for the origin of individual human, rational souls.

As we have seen, Alexander designed his interpretation as a defence of Aristotle's apparent claim that time could not exist without soul. Yet we must now briefly consider to what extent his own solution remained faithful to the broader contours of Aristotle's philosophy of time. After all, Boethus had rejected the codependency of time and soul in the interest of affirming a genuinely Aristotelian ontology. Does Alexander's interpretative defence of the Stagirite, then, constitute a pyrrhic victory or does it do justice to the intellectual impulse in Aristotle's own approach?

This question is not rhetorical. As we saw at the beginning of this account, Aristotle's theory of time was developed against the view of time as an image of eternity as found in the *Timaeus*. Key for Aristotle was a definition of time as directly related to change. Time ought to be understood in connection with the various movements that make up the physical world; insofar as they occur within what he called a 'before-and-after structure' they occur within time. The definition of time as 'number' therefore was decidedly *not* meant as an idealistic account in which time once again became an intelligible reality detached from physical changes although, admittedly, it was much more difficult to ascertain quite *what* it was meant to be.

There is no doubt that Alexander's reconstruction pushes Aristotle's original account closer to that of the *Timaeus* than previous Peripatetics had done. The question is how closely he aligned it with the Platonic theory and whether he was able to retain the original intuition that had motivated Aristotle's opposition to the cosmology of his erstwhile teacher. It seems to me that the decisive criterion in answering this question must be whether or not Alexander retained a notion of time (and of physics more generally) as fundamentally tied to our experience or whether he reverted back to a philosophy for which the world of our experience could only be approached by means of reflections on a reality that, by definition, transcends it.

With reference to time and soul, the question may be phrased as follows: does the stipulation of a cosmic soul as the basis of movement and time stabilise and explain the reality of time as 'counted' by our own rational souls? Or does reference to the world soul make time, ultimately, a property of that cosmic soul which is present only secondarily in the physical world? The former answer would, I think, be a legitimate interpretation of Aristotle and furthermore represent a plausible exegesis of the *aporia* from Physics IV 14; the latter answer, by contrast, would mark the transition into a Platonic framework which could not any longer be truly reconciled with Aristotle's own thought.

There are good reasons to ascribe to Alexander the former of these two views, but it will also become apparent in what follows how he prepared the ground for the latter view *as an interpretation of Aristotle*. For the problem of time and soul, in any event, I would suggest that Alexander's reading holds the 'subjective' and the 'objective' in the balance as long as we accept that the two parts of his response to Boethus have the same weight. In this case, Alexander would fundamentally insist that the subjective perception of time is essential for the being of time while referring to the universal soul as a background theory needed to underwrite the reality of this experience, but not to replace it.

3 Soul and Time in Neoplatonist Interpretations of Aristotle

The direct line of the ancient interpretation of Aristotle's *aporia* leads from Alexander to the sixth-century philosopher, Simplicius of Cilicia, who offers the most extensive interpretation of Aristotle's *aporia*.[1] Simplicius in many ways is Alexander's successor as the paradigmatic commentator. As the second-century Peripatetic scholar, his Neoplatonic counterpart is incredibly learned and pays scrupulous attention to his texts. Yet the three centuries that separate the two scholars brought important changes to the philosophical world of late antiquity. For once, they saw the Christianisation of the Roman Empire. In fact, Simplicius belonged to the last generation of Neoplatonists who still worked at the School of Athens before it was closed by imperial edict in 529. The significance of this transformation will have to be considered in the next chapter.

In terms more specifically of the philosophical tradition, the century following the life of Alexander witnessed the rise of a novel form of Platonism, which today we call Neoplatonism. Neoplatonism soon became the single, dominant philosophical school in the Greek-speaking world. With its twin centres of Athens and Alexandria, Neoplatonism continued its philosophical reign for a remarkable three hundred years during which time it exerted considerable influence on Latin as well as nascent Syriac thought, not to mention its complex relationship with the emerging Christian tradition.

It is thus immediately evident that Neoplatonism, although neglected in Western philosophical historiography for a long time, was one of the most successful philosophical movements ever. Part of the explanation for this extraordinary success must be seen in the fact that it was able to integrate major tenets of its competitor schools, especially those held by Stoics and Peripatetics. This is all the more remarkable in view of the fact that Neoplatonism was by no means an attempt at compromise or rapprochement between the various philosophical traditions. It was not syncretism or eclecticism that permitted the integration of rival insights but the creation of a philosophical perspective from which alternative philosophies could appear as legitimate while restricted in the range of their theoretical insights.

This visionary philosophy was not the product of a single individual, but it is arguable that the single most important contribution towards its creation was

---

[1] The *aporia* is also briefly commented on by Themistius and Philoponus. Cf. Jeck 1994, 26–36 (Themistius) and 60–70 (Philoponus).

that of Plotinus (c. 205–270). Plotinus, who was brought up in Egypt but later taught philosophy at Rome, is highly unusual among late ancient philosophers in that his literary production was not directly the result of his interaction with classical texts. Unlike Alexander or his own student, Porphyry, Plotinus does not, for example, seem to have written commentaries. This is not to say, however, that his own philosophy, which we have in a remarkably coherent corpus of thirty-six writings transmitted in six groups of nine treatises, the so-called *Enneads*, did not grow out of the engagement with previous philosophers. Plotinus taught philosophy in a school. We know from his biography, written by his student Porphyry, that the teaching in Plotinus' school was based on the textual study of a wide range of previous philosophical writings including the works of Plato, Aristotle, and Alexander.[2]

It was Porphyry (234?-305?) who resumed the practice we have encountered in Alexander of developing philosophy through commentary, and Porphyry is therefore the proper originator of the Neoplatonic commentary tradition among whose main authorities on the exegetical side was none other than Alexander of Aphrodisias. Yet Porphyry's work would have been impossible had not Plotinus himself initiated the project of Neoplatonism as a renewal of Plato's philosophy which could, at the same time, integrate important insights from the other schools. In fact, Porphyry is insistent that 'Stoic and Peripatetic doctrines' are absorbed into Plotinus' thought and that Aristotle's *Metaphysics* in particular is present across his writings.[3]

The details of this terse statement have been increasingly elucidated by recent research which has, consequently, shown that there is both continuity and discontinuity in Plotinus' thought and that, therefore, the use of the term Neoplatonism for the kind of philosophy that started, to our knowledge, with him, must not occlude his debt to thinkers prior to him. And yet, it would be equally problematic to overlook the radical nature of the reorientation of philosophy that happened with Plotinus and gave to the subsequent philosophical movement its unique and characteristic direction.[4] It is for this reason that Plotinus must briefly be discussed in connection within the present investigation.

---

2 Porphyry, *Vita Plotini* 14.
3 Ibid.
4 Cf. Chiaradonna 2013, 52 with n. 89 for a judicious assessment of the *status quaestionis*.

Plotinus on time and soul

As it happens, Plotinus himself wrote a full treatise on the problem of time. It is easily argued that, after Aristotle, he was the most important and the most influential philosopher in antiquity to attempt an answer to the problem of what time is. According to Porphyry's list of Plotinus' works, the treatise bears the title *On time and eternity*; and whether or not this was Plotinus' own title, it certainly characterises the work well. In Porphyry's edition the treatise is the seventh writing in the third *Ennead* (III 7); we are also told that chronologically it was the forty-ninth work of Plotinus dating from the very end of Porphyry's time with his master.[5]

The text is important in the present context for a number of reasons. First of all, Plotinus clearly seeks to reassert the concept of time underlying the *Timaeus* and develop Plato's rather sketchy account into a viable more comprehensive theory of time. As such, Plotinus' argument is inevitably critical of Aristotle's account. After all, Aristotle himself had been primarily motivated, as we saw, by a sense that Plato's explanation of time as an 'image of eternity' was not answering the questions we should ask about time. Plotinus, by contrast, clearly agrees with the fundamental intuition that time (and the visible world in its entirety) can only be satisfactorily explained by grounding it in transcendent reality. The world of our experience, on this view, will only become intelligible to us by being understood as a reflection of an ontologically more perfect world, the *kosmos noētos*.

What to Aristotle, then, had seemed the chief weakness of Plato's account, appeared to Plotinus its major strength, and his entire project, therefore, had to involve a kind of metacritique of Aristotle in order to accomplish its ultimate purpose. Time *cannot* be explained on the basis of our observation of change in the physical world. Again and again, Plotinus insists that any such attempt moves around in a circle presupposing what it aims to prove.[6] The reason is that, according to Plotinus, the empirical world as a whole is always already *in time* and cannot therefore offer us an angle from which to understand it. Such an angle is only gained by taking our position from outside time, and this precisely is why Plotinus *begins* his account with reflections on eternity.[7]

---

5 Porphyry, *Vita Plotini* 5. *Ennead* III 7 has been extensively studied. Cf. Beierwaltes 1967; McGuire/Strange 1988; Tempest-Walters 2019 (with extensive bibliography).
6 Cf. his criticism of earlier theories in *Ennead* III 7, 7–8.
7 Plotinus, *Ennead* III 7, 1, 16–7.

While this opposition to Aristotle is undoubtedly a main and recurrent feature throughout the text of *Ennead* III 7 and especially in section 9 which is specifically devoted to the discussion of *Physics* IV 10–14, it would nevertheless be facile to reduce Plotinus' engagement with the Stagirite to the level of critique or rejection.[8] As we have seen, Aristotle's account of time was not purely empirical or, at least, it did not have to be understood in such a way. Specifically, its key feature, the identification of time as number (Plotinus, to be sure, prefers the term 'measure'[9]), could appear as indicating a move away from an exclusively physical account of time. Time for Aristotle was not change it was 'of change'; *in a qualified sense* Plotinus could agree with that as he too believed that time was limited to the physical universe in which change existed.

Finally, a word needs to be said about Plotinus' own definition of time as the 'life of the Soul'.[10] This is by no means a simple restatement of Plato's theory which, in any event, was inchoate at best.[11] Rather, it is a sophisticated novel development without a clear precedent in previous Platonism. One notable novelty of this theory is the important role Soul plays for it. Soul, here, means the third level of Plotinus' hierarchical ontology, an intelligible 'hypostasis' located between the Intellect and sensible reality. The introduction of Soul in this sense was one of Plotinus' most momentous philosophical innovations. Plotinus' Soul is not the world soul but universal being in which individual souls, human as well as non-human, participate and of which they are parts. The Soul grounds psychic reality in the empirical world in its own ontological principle.[12]

Plotinus' reference to Soul as the originator of time, then, indicates that his main interest in time may be called psychological. It is, *nota bene*, not psychological in the sense that time would be subjective, but it ties time to the existence of psychic reality in the world, rather than the reality of physical or cosmological movements as had been the case in much of the earlier tradition. To be sure, Plotinus does not deny the cosmic dimension of time or its relevance; Soul, after all, is directly responsible for the existence of the physical universe including its temporality.[13] Yet despite its connection with the sensible universe, the Soul, as its name suggests, is first and foremost connected with individual souls.

---

8 On Plotinus' relationship to Aristotle in general cf. Magrin 2016.
9 Plotinus, *Ennead* III 7, 9, 1.
10 Plotinus, *Ennead* III 7, 11, 44–5.
11 Plotinus echoes Plato's words at III 7, 11, 20: '… we produced time as the image of eternity.' ET: McGuire/Strange, 262.
12 Cf. now Caluori 2015 for a full account of this important aspect of Plotinus' thought.
13 Caluori 2015, 25–36.

Plotinus thus should have had quite some sympathies for Aristotle's claim that there can be no time without soul; it is therefore intriguing to observe that he comments on the *aporia*, if only briefly. What can be gleaned from these remarks?

Plotinus on Aristotle's *aporia*

Plotinus does not offer a commentary on Aristotle's treatise on time. In fact, it has been observed that his engagement with Aristotle's text is rather slapdash focussing mostly on the Stagirite's definition of time in IV 11.[14] His comments on the *aporia* follow this pattern. Plotinus does not cite Aristotle's text and his response is given in a rapid succession of extremely abbreviated and elliptical sentences. Yet the fact that he deemed the *aporia* worthy of mention in the first instance is significant warranting a closer analysis of the relevant text.

The passage is to be found at the very end of *Ennead* III 7, 9, the section in which Plotinus deals with Aristotle's theory of time. It reads as follows:

> But why will time not also exist prior to the soul that measures it? Unless one says that it arises from the soul. Yet it is not in any way necessary that the soul exists to measure it, for it exists with the extent it has even if no one measures it. Someone might say that it is the soul which uses magnitude to measure time. But how could this help with the conception of time?[15]

The text is typical of Plotinus' generally dismissive mode of engagement with Aristotle throughout the whole section. The first sentence seems to reject out of hand Aristotle's claim that time cannot exist without a soul counting it. This rejection is part of Plotinus' general strategy in the section to push back against Aristotle's definition. Time *as* number or measure cannot explain anything because it relies on phenomena which already presuppose temporality.

And yet, it appears that as much as his criticism is targeted against the idea of soul as counting or measuring time, it is also limited to that aspect of Aristotle's *aporia*. It is this specific line of argument which, as we have seen, Boethus had already rejected from a Peripatetic point of view, that stands at the centre of

---

14 Clark 1944, 344.
15 Plotinus, *Ennead* III 7, 9, 78–84. ET: McGuire/Strange, 261: Διὰ τί δὲ οὐκ ἔσται πρὶν καὶ ψυχὴν τὴν μετροῦσαν εἶναι; Εἰ μή τις τὴν γένεσιν αὐτοῦ παρὰ ψυχῆς λέγοι γίνεσθαι. Ἐπεὶ διά γε τὸ μετρεῖν οὐδαμῶς ἀναγκαῖον εἶναι· ὑπάρχει γὰρ ὅσον ἐστί, κἂν μή τις μετρῇ. Τὸ δὲ τῷ μεγέθει χρησάμενον πρὸς τὸ μετρῆσαι τὴν ψυχὴν ἄν τις λέγοι· τοῦτο δὲ τί ἂν εἴη πρὸς ἔννοιαν χρόνου;

Plotinus' critique. As for the rest, Plotinus allows or even expects his readers to go below the surface of his critique.

The first sentence already seems ambiguous. While it might seem to suggest that time existed prior to any soul that may count it, Plotinus' belief in the eternal existence of souls should caution against any interpretation that would commit him to a temporal beginning of the soul. What he rather seems to suggest is that time always precedes any counting act in which the soul may be engaged. Time existed before the soul 'insofar as it measures it' might be a translation of Plotinus' dense text bringing out this meaning.

Such an understanding makes the transition to his next statement plausible. Of course, the reader of Plotinus' treatise knows (or will find out) that soul *does* produce or generate time.[16] It is therefore correct, according to Plotinus, to say that time cannot exist without soul and that soul exists 'before' time, but this priority cannot be asserted on the basis of soul *qua* numbering. The same argument is extended in the remainder of the passage. Measuring time is not 'necessary' for its existence; it exists as what it is even when no one is measuring it.

It is interesting that Plotinus, thus far, agrees with Boethus who had likewise rejected Aristotle's suggestion that time as something countable could only exist if there was also someone counting it. Alexander's response, if Plotinus knew it, does not seem to have swayed his position at all. Yet this does not mean that there is no trace of Alexander's argument in Plotinus' discussion of the *aporia*. After all, we have seen that Alexander himself added to the discussion about the problem by suggesting that time was dependent on soul on a cosmic scale. In his case, it is true, the argument seemed to rest primarily on the idea that soul was the cause of all change and movement in the world and thus also of time. Yet the idea that Aristotle's *aporia* could be solved by stipulating an ontological dependency of time on soul to explain the noetic dependency of which the Stagirite seemed to speak, connects the Peripatetic and the Neoplatonist philosophers.

It is, therefore, possible to inscribe Plotinus' reading of the *aporia* into a trajectory beginning with Alexander. This trajectory was started, I would argue, by Alexander's decision to underwrite Aristotle's claim about the dependency of time on soul by a reference to the cosmic soul as the universal cause of movement. Plotinus follows that hint and can find agreement with Aristotle insofar as he is capable of being understood along those lines. It is intriguing in this connection to note that Plotinus concedes the possibility that the *Physics* was meant for people who 'had heard [Aristotle's] lectures'[17] and that its teaching

---

16 Plotinus, *Ennead* III 7, 11, 15–20.
17 Plotinus, *Ennead* III 7, 13, 16–8.

was therefore liable to being misunderstood. Although this is, in Plotinus' text, specifically applied to the distinction between time as measure and time as being measured,[18] it is tempting to find here a more general acceptance of an interpretation such as Alexander's which read Aristotle's comments on time and soul in light of the Stagirite's cosmological and metaphysical principles as expressed elsewhere in his works.

This does not make Plotinus agree wholeheartedly with either Aristotle or Alexander. He *does* reject the definition of time as number, and Aristotle's claim that time needs someone to count it to him, therefore, merely illustrates the futility of such an approach. His understanding of Soul as the originator of time, on the other hand, is less mechanical than Alexander's. In fact, there are indications in Plotinus' treatise that might suggest that for him the origin of time lies primarily with *individual* souls rather than the cosmic Soul.[19] Although this interpretation is not consensual, it indicates that Plotinus' theory of time has a *subjective*, experiential dimension which, I have argued, Aristotle's view had as well but which was largely sidelined in the subsequent history of interpretation. This subjective dimension, however, for Plotinus was the futile and tragic decision to turn away from the happiness to be found in the now in favour of a treacherous hope to betterment through temporal progression[20] whereas for Aristotle it consisted in the experiential basis from which our awareness of time cannot be abstracted.

How much of all this must be explained through literary dependency and how much is more a matter of intellectual development is hard to adjudicate in a thinker as deeply steeped in philosophical learning but also startlingly original as Plotinus. What is important, in any event, is to recognise that the discussion of time and soul takes on a new direction in Neoplatonism. The main feature of this new departure is Plotinus' decision to tie the ontological origin of time to Soul. For those Neoplatonists who returned to the tradition of writing full commentaries on Aristotle, this decision had far-reaching consequences in their appropriation of the Stagirite's teaching within a Neoplatonic context. For Plotinus' Christian readers on the other hand, to whom I will turn in my next chapter, this decision became relevant in a rather different but equally significant way.

---

18 Cf. Aristotle, *Physics* IV 12 (220b32–221a9).
19 Tempest-Walters 2019, 93–4 and passim.
20 *Ibid.*

Simplicius' Commentary on Aristotle's *Physics*

Simplicius of Cilicia belongs to the last generation of Neoplatonist philosophers teaching at the Academy of Athens until its closure by Emperor Justinian I in 529.[21] At that time, Simplicius and six of his colleagues left the Empire for Persia in order to avoid conversion to Christianity, but they returned a few years later, apparently with the guarantee to be able to continue in their traditional ways.[22] Apart from that, we know very little about him. He seems to have studied both at Alexandria and at Athens before taking up his teaching post at the latter of those two schools.

Like Alexander three hundred years before him, Simplicius developed his philosophical thought primarily through commentaries. In many ways, he is for Neoplatonism what Alexander was for the Peripatos, the paradigmatic commentator. The main difference is that a number of Simplicius' major commentaries are extant and so we have first-hand evidence of his impressive learning, his interpretative skills, his even-handed approach to the texts, and his own philosophical sophistication which was considerable.[23]

Simplicius has often been studied for his citations from earlier authors whose writings are now lost.[24] While it is today recognised that a purely source-critical approach to his commentaries does not do justice to their philosophical quality, it remains a remarkable fact quite how much of traditional ancient philosophical thought Simplicius took into account in his own philosophising. From the Presocratics to the major Hellenistic schools to the earlier commentary literature, there are not many names he seems to have skipped in his attempt to grapple with a given problem. He clearly aspired to be as comprehensive as possible; the sheer bulk of his commentaries shows to what lengths he went in that attempt.[25]

Simplicius' *Commentary on Aristotle's Physics* is undoubtedly one of his most momentous achievements. Through a detailed engagement with the Aristotelian writing, the author ultimately presents a grand vision of Greek natural philosophy from its inception in the Presocratics, based on a Neoplatonic perspective.[26]

---

21 On Simplicius' life and works the fullest account remains Hadot 1987.
22 Baltussen 2008, 12–3 who aptly describes this episode as a 'hotly debated topic'.
23 For Simplicius as an exegete cf. the full study by Baltussen 2008.
24 Baltussen 2008, 4.
25 Baltussen 2008, 2.
26 Note with Barney (2009, 104) that Simplicius does exclude some groups of thinkers from his synthesis, 'notably the Epicureans and sceptics'. Barney also, helpfully, points out how impor-

Most of his discussion is conducted in a line-by-line commentary on Aristotle's text, but in a few cases Simplicius inserted small dissertations, 'corollaries' that present his own considered view of the matter although even there his reasoning is conducted in constant exchange with the views of earlier generations of philosophers.

One of these corollaries is dedicated to the topic of time.[27] While Simplicius' full discussion of Aristotle's *aporia* is to be found in his commentary on *Physics* IV 14, it is worthwhile beginning our examination of Simplicius' treatment of time and soul in this place. Simplicius leaves no doubt that he regards Plotinus as the major turning point in the history of philosophical reflections on time.[28] Plotinus, he argues, was the first to recognise that time properly speaking belongs to the realm of Soul; physical time can only be understood if seen from this vantage point. Simplicius here ascribes to Plotinus a distinction which is, actually, only found in the later Neoplatonist Iamblichus of Chalcis, who in this connection had spoken of a 'first time' (πρῶτος χρόνος).[29]

Despite this acknowledgment of Plotinus' pivotal role, however, Simplicius does not repeat the polemics against earlier thinkers we have found in *Ennead* III 7. The reason for that is simple and straightforward. As is evident from Simplicius' account, he thinks that *all* philosophers prior to Plotinus only dealt with physical time.[30] What they said, in other words, about time and the movement of the sphere of fixed stars, was not wrong; it was merely incomplete and therefore gains its full sense when seen in the perspective opened up by Neoplatonist speculation.

This argument is characteristic of Simplicius' approach; as we shall see in what follows, he applies it equally when commenting on points of detail in Aristotle's text. It is a brilliant methodology capable of integrating the wealth of previous Greek philosophical reflection without obscuring differences and distinctions. Simplicius does not, as far as I see, comment directly on Plotinus' dismissive remarks concerning Aristotle's views on time, but he certainly had an answer to the problem. Plotinus was not wrong to distance his own philosophy from that of the Stagirite, but their difference, in the end, was better explained as a difference in the kind of question they asked and the kind of explanation

---

tant Simplicius' radically anti-Christian attitude is for his presentation of a harmony between the older Greek tradition (*ibid.*).

27 A detailed discussion of this text in Sonderegger 1982.
28 Simplicius, *In Aristotelis physicorum libros commentaria* (790, 26–31 Diels). Cf. Sonderegger 1982, 82.
29 Simplicius, *In Aristotelis physicorum libros commentaria* (792, 21–3 Diels).
30 Simplicius, *In Aristotelis physicorum libros commentaria* (790, 26–31 Diels).

they sought. On his own terms, Aristotle was almost entirely right, and what is missing from his treatise is absent because it fell outside its scope.

How could such an assessment be justified? Intriguingly, Simplicius refers to Aristotle's *aporia* within the *Corollary*, more specifically at the end of his discussion of Plotinus' theory of time. Having established that Plotinus' definition of time as the 'life of the Soul' refers to the 'basic' or first time as 'the one that measures the changing life of the soul', he continues as follows:

> Perhaps this is the point that Aristotle seized on when he said that there would be no time if there were no soul, because there was nothing that made the count. So let time have its basis in the soul, though it is something additional to soul that measures its changing activity.[31]

It is remarkable what has happened here. Alexander had introduced the idea that time depends on soul in the sense that time depends on change which, in its turn, depends on the cosmic soul. Plotinus went a step further and made time in general dependent on Soul, understood as a unified intelligible reality. Simplicius follows Plotinus, but is willing to accept Aristotle's original determination of the soul as 'counting' time as applying to the pre-cosmic, intelligible time which exists as the life of the Soul, more precisely as the measure of its 'changing activity'.

This willingness to let Aristotle's view stand in its entirety while, apparently, giving to it an interpretation far removed from its original intention, namely, as part of a Neoplatonic theory of primary time will also emerge from Simplicius' treatment of the *aporia* in his commentary on *Physics* IV. Yet the fact that Simplicius references the passage where he sums up his interpretation of Plotinus shows how important it was for his interpretation of Aristotle as well as his own understanding of time.

Simplicius on Aristotle's *aporia*

Simplicius' commentary on the *aporia* extends over more than two pages in Diels' edition of the Greek text and over nearly three pages in Urmson's English translation. The length of the passage is due in part, however, to Simplicius'

---

31 Simplicius, *In Aristotelis physicorum libros commentaria* (792, 26–31 Diels). ET: Urmson 1992a, 113: καὶ τοῦτο τάχα ἐστίν, οὗ καὶ Ἀριστοτέλης ἐφαψάμενος ἔλεγε μὴ εἶναι χρόνον, εἰ μὴ εἴη ψυχή, διότι μὴ ἔστι τὸ ἀριθμοῦν. ἀρχέσθω μὲν οὖν ἀπὸ τῆς ψυχῆς ὁ χρόνος, ἄλλος δὲ ὢν παρὰ τὴν ψυχὴν καὶ τὰς μεταβολικὰς αὐτῆς μετρῶν ἐνεργείας.

practice of referring in detail to earlier commentators. In this case, the two earlier scholars he mentions are Boethus and Alexander. In fact, their interpretations of Aristotle's text which were analysed above are known to us largely through Simplicius' detailed account of their views.

In this connection it is interesting that one major part of Alexander's argument, his reference to the cosmic soul as the source of all movement and thus, indirectly, of time, is only linked to Alexander by Simplicius in an oblique manner. Prior to the edition of the *Scholia* to Alexander's own *Commentary* it might have been natural to think of this section as Simplicius' own, Platonising reading of Aristotle's *aporia*.[32] This indicates that the precise extent of Simplicius' debt to previous interpreters and, by implication, the exact limitations of Simplicius' own commentary are impossible to determine in view of the fact that most of his sources are lost to us.

That said, Simplicius' commentary on the Aristotelian passage seems to fall rather conveniently into three parts: (1) an initial restatement of Aristotle's argument which may or may not be Simplicius' own; (2) an account of the debate between Boethus and Alexander which he took probably from the latter's *Commentary on the Physics*; (3) his own interpretation.

The first part (758, 30 – 759, 16) is a careful reconstruction of what Aristotle is claiming. Simplicius follows Alexander in understanding 'that which counts' and 'that which is counted' as relatives which can only exist together. Having dealt with some questions of detail,[33] Simplicius offers the following summary of Aristotle's argument:

> So the entire process of drawing to a conclusion in three stages runs as follows: if there is nothing which will enumerate, nor is there the enumerable; but if there is nothing enumerable there is no number *qua* enumerable. So if what will enumerate is the soul through its intelligence and time is number, if there were no soul there would be no time.[34]

---

32 Simplicius, *In Aristotelis physicorum libros commentaria* (760, 14 – 26 Diels). Cf. Rashed 2011, 288 – 9. In what follows, in-line citations refer to Diels' edition of Simplicius' commentary. The English text quoted follows Urmson 1992. For Simplicius' interpretation of the *aporia* cf. also Jeck 1994, 37 – 59.
33 E.g.: Should Aristotle have used the term 'that which counts' rather than 'that which will count'? (759, 5 – 9 Diels).
34 Simplicius, *In Aristotelis physicorum libros commentaria* (759, 14 – 7 Diels). ET: Urmson 1992, 172 (with changes): ὥστε ἡ ὅλη συναγωγὴ κατὰ τὴν διὰ τριῶν ἀγωγὴν τοιαύτη· εἰ μὴ τὸ ἀριθμῆσον, οὐδὲ τὸ ἀριθμητόν· εἰ μὴ τὸ ἀριθμητόν, οὐδὲ ἀριθμὸς ὁ ὡς ἀριθμητός· εἰ οὖν τὸ μὲν ἀριθμῆσον ψυχὴ κατὰ τὸν ἑαυτῆς νοῦν, ὁ δὲ χρόνος ἀριθμός, μὴ οὔσης ψυχῆς οὐκ ἂν εἴη χρόνος.

Note that this reconstruction only considers the first part of the *aporia*, the question of whether the character of time as number implies a logical dependency of time on soul and, consequently an ontological dependency as well. The subsequent problem of whether the 'substrate of time' or change could exist without soul (and its connection with the initial *aporia*) is left to one side here.

Subsequent to this exposition of the problem, Simplicius recounts in detail the controversy between Boethus and Alexander, which I will skip here as both positions have been discussed in detail in the previous chapter. It is clear that Simplicius sides with Alexander both in his concession to Boethus and, more importantly, in his solution of the problem 'in accordance with Aristotle', as Simplicius notes (759, 21). Despite restricting his original exposition of the *aporia* to its first part, Simplicius seems to follow Alexander in transitioning to the question of whether change could exist without soul.

Due to our dearth of source, it is here not entirely easy to see where Alexander's words end and where Simplicius' begin. Simplicius at any rate commits himself to the view that Aristotle's conditional statement 'if it is possible for change to exist without soul' must be understood as conceding that 'so far as the antithesis of relations goes' (ἐπὶ τῇ κατὰ τὰ πρός τι ἀντιθέσει) it is indeed correct that change could exist without soul (760, 12–3). In other words, while *time* logically requires the existence of soul, change does not. In the 'real world', however, this possibility does not obtain, as Alexander, whose words Simplicius now follows, has shown: 'if soul were abolished all change would be abolished' (ἀναιρουμένης ψυχῆς ἀναιροῖτο ἂν πᾶσα κίνησις: 760, 18).[35]

From 760, 27, the final section of the commentary begins, which apparently presents Simplicius' own view.[36] Here, the author introduces a distinction in Aristotle's concept of time. From the definition ('the number of change with regard to before and after') he deduces that there is time *qua* 'number of change' and time *qua* 'before and after'. Insofar as time is the 'enumerated number' (ἀριθμὸς ἀριθμητός : 760, 28), it is indeed done away with in the absence of someone who counts. Insofar as it is 'the before and after with regard to the duration in which change exists' (κατὰ τὴν τοῦ εἶναι τῆς κινήσεως παράτασιν: 760, 28–30), it continues to exist even without someone who counts. In this regard, Simplicius argues, its character as something that is counted is accidental.

---

[35] Note that this is practically identical with Ursula Coope's interpretation of Aristotle's text: there *could* be a world with change but without soul, but there cannot be one with time but no soul. In reality, or in Aristotelian reality, there is, however, no world without soul: Coope 2005, 162–3.

[36] He introduces it with ὡς οἶμαι.

It is only when the soul is seen in its role as the 'principle of becoming and of all change in regard to becoming' (ἀρχὴ γενέσεώς ἐστι καὶ τῆς κατὰ τὴν γένεσιν πάσης κινήσεως: 760, 32) that we fully grasp the dependency of time on soul. Soul *in this understanding*, that is in its cosmic function, is the originator of time in the fullest sense. Simplicius thus draws two distinctions: between soul *qua* counting and soul *qua* the 'principle of becoming'; and between time as enumerated number and time as the extension of changeable being. As much as the cosmic, universal soul is the ontologically prior reality which sustains and explains the existence and the functions of the empirical, individual soul, as much is time as extension of changeable being more comprehensive and more foundational than time as number.

We find here, in other words, a reappearance of Plotinus' objections to the notion that time should be 'number'.[37] True to style, Simplicius does not present this idea as one absolutely to be rejected, but there is no doubt that he agrees with the founder of Neoplatonism that it is inferior and needs serious improvement. As is evident throughout his commentary on Aristotle's treatise on time, Simplicius is at pains to present the Stagirite as having himself held a different view, namely, that time is the measure of flow and extension in their true being.[38] Thus he concludes a lengthy discussion earlier in his *Commentary* with the following words:

> Time is the measure of the flow and the extension of existence. [...] This, as seems to me, is the penetrating and apposite philosophical teaching of Aristotle about time.[39]

It is time thus understood which, according to Simplicius, has countability only accidentally and can therefore continue to exist without being counted. It is, likewise, time in this sense which owes its being to Soul as the 'principle of becoming and of all change in regard to becoming'.

It is furthermore intriguing that Simplicius' distinction between these two aspects of time apparently facilitates a vindication of sorts for Boethus' criticism of Aristotle's *aporia* as well as a remarkable reconciliation of his and Alexander's conflicting arguments. Simplicius, for whom everyone seems to possess some partial truth, can uphold Boethus' criticism insofar as it applies to time as the

---

37 Plotinus, *Ennead* III 7, 9, 1.
38 Cf. Sonderegger 1982, 40.
39 Simplicius, *In Aristotelis physicorum libros commentaria* (738, 2–5 Diels). ET: Urmson 1992, 148: καὶ οὕτως ὁ χρόνος μέτρον τῆς κατὰ τὸ εἶναι ῥοῆς καὶ παρατάσεώς ἐστι. καὶ ταῦτά ἐστιν, ὡς ἐμοὶ δοκεῖ, τὰ νοερῶς καὶ εὐεπηβόλως παραδοθέντα τοῦ Ἀριστοτέλους φιλοσοφήματα περὶ τοῦ χρόνου.

'before and after with regard to the duration in which change exists'. Should he (like Paul Moraux[40]), have thought that Boethus rejected Aristotle's definition of time as number in the first instance, such an interpretation would have appeared even more plausible.

Alexander's logical defence of Aristotle's position, on the other hand, would be correct (and presumably a better interpretation of Aristotle insofar as it absolved him of the kind of mistake diagnosed by Boethus and Plotinus), but only valid as far as it goes, namely, as applied to time as 'enumerated number' and thus to *one*, rather limited aspect of time. Both Boethus and Alexander are therefore right, each in their own way. Yet there is little doubt that for Simplicius the value of Alexander's rejoinder of the countable *as* countable that does not exist without someone counting is more dialectical than speculative.

Within Alexander's twofold argument, Simplicius thus unambiguously prioritises its second part in which time was established as dependent on the cosmic soul as the origin of all cosmic movement and change. Unlike Plotinus, the Neoplatonic commentator does not explicitly dismiss the justification of time as dependent on the counting soul, but this is more a matter of style than substance. Ultimately, both Neoplatonists agree that the relationship of time and soul is only correctly conceived if applied to the ontological relationship between Soul as an intelligible hypostasis and time as the ordered structure of the sensible world.

In this sense, Simplicius concludes his interpretation of Aristotle's *aporia* by noting his agreement with Plato:

> Note how here, also, Aristotle wrote in accord with our leader. He himself wrote 'if it is possible for there to be change without soul', i.e. without the changer, while the other said that for other things that change the soul is the 'source and principle',[41] and that from that principle everything in becoming comes to be.[42]

It is then clear that Simplicius in a way marks the end of the trajectory that began with Alexander. While the latter had defended against Boethus' critique Aristotle's thesis that time as number needs a soul for counting it, he had

---

40 Moraux 1973–2001, vol. 1, 171.
41 Cf. Plato, *Phaedrus* 245c.
42 Simplicius, *In Aristotelis physicorum libros commentaria* (761, 5–8 Diels). ET: Urmson 1992, 174: ὅρα ὅπως κἀνταῦθα σύμφωνα γέγραφεν ὁ Ἀριστοτέλης τῷ σφετέρῳ καθηγεμόνι αὐτὸς εἰπὼν εἰ ἐνδέχεται κίνησιν εἶναι ἄνευ ψυχῆς, τουτέστιν ἄνευ τοῦ κινοῦντος, ἐκείνῳ λέγοντι ὅτι τοῖς ἄλλοις ὅσα κινεῖται "πηγὴ καὶ ἀρχὴ κινήσεώς" ἐστιν ἡ ψυχή, καὶ ὅτι ἐξ ἀρχῆς ταύτης πᾶν τὸ γινόμενον γίνεται.

also introduced the subsidiary argument that time depends on the cosmic soul as the origin of all change. Plotinus could be understood as rejecting the former of these arguments while building on the latter to claim that time was generated by the universal soul alongside the visible cosmos in its entirety. Being unabashedly polemical with regard to Aristotle's definition of time as number, all that remained of value in the Stagirite's theory was, it seems, the intimation that time depended on soul in its existence.

At the same time, the founder of Neoplatonism emphasised the psychological features inherent in time so much so that some interpreters find him advocating the view that physical time ultimately is the product of individual souls in their turning away from happiness in the eternal now. In other words, while seemingly drawing on Alexander's cosmological link between soul and time, his own conception of Soul shifts the logic of this argument away from a source of movement and change to the paradigm of psychic activity.

In Simplicius, by contrast, this shift seems to be reversed. While avoiding the combative tone characteristic of *Ennead* III 7, his own marginalisation of time as number and the consequent restriction of Alexander's defence of Aristotle's claim to this subaltern aspect of time gives to Aristotle's *aporia* a meaning that is practically devoid of any subjective dimension. Time, it seems, is part of a complex ontological movement from unity to plurality. It enters into this process on the initiative of the Soul and, in that sense, cannot exist without soul. Soul, however, seems to be reduced here to the kind of cosmological function ascribed to it in Alexander's Peripatetic logic.

Thus far, Aristotle's argument seems to be turned on its head even though it is, apparently, fully affirmed by Simplicius. The basis of time in our own experience of physical change seems to have entirely disappeared from view in favour of an objectivised process into which the reality of soul is somehow integrated.

What, finally, do we make of Simplicius' reference to the *aporia* in his *Corollary on Time?* In light of his commentary on the Aristotelian passage, this hint must appear puzzling. After all, he had spent much interpretative effort to argue that the notion of time as number was marginal in Aristotle's own account and that the value of his *aporia* was only properly understood when it was referred to the universal soul as the source of all physical movement. It is, then, remarkable that *after* all that he throws out a hint to his readers that there may be a greater significance to the Stagirite's proposal after all that, namely, time as number could be applied to the first or basic time which exists together with the universal soul.

There may, then, be a final, ironic twist in Simplicius' argument in that the notion of time as depending on the soul's counting, which was deemed insufficient at the physical level, gains its true meaning and importance at the intelligible level. It would chime with Simplicius' overall conviction that Aristotle knew and approved the (Neo-)Platonic theory of time but intentionally restricted himself to an explication of its physical dimension. Quite how far he was willing to pursue this interpretation or what consequences, if any, it would have for his interpretation of physical time, must however remain open due to the absence of further textual evidence.

4 Time and Soul in Patristic Thought

The discussion of Aristotle's *aporia* among Neoplatonist led, as we have seen in the previous chapter, to an interpretation for which the subjective dimension of time had become all but dispensable. While Simplicius affirmed that time could not exist without soul, he explained this through the metaphysical link between the universal soul and the physical world offering, in effect, a Platonising reading of an argument first advanced by Alexander of Aphrodisias. At the same time, the recognition of the importance of subjective or experiential time, which seems to have been present in Alexander and which, for partly different reasons, was affirmed by Plotinus as well, appears reduced to utter marginality in Simplicius.

There exists, however, a second ending of the same narrative which is to be found in some Christian authors. Their inclusion in the present account, admittedly, has to be justified. To begin with, there is no direct evidence, to the best of my knowledge, for the use of Aristotle's *aporia* (or indeed his treatise on time) among Christian authors until the sixth century at the earliest. What is more, interest in subjective time or even the relationship between time and soul is also exceedingly rare in early Christian literature. There is, of course, the case of St Augustin, arguably the most prominent representative of such an approach to time in the whole of ancient thought, but his ideas on this topic seem to be the product of his personal genius more than the result of an intellectual tradition.

And yet, there are good reasons to include early Christian reflection on time into the present book's narrative. The first of these is based on the link, which has often been noted, between Augustine's view of time and Plotinus *Ennead* III 7.[1] To the extent that the latter text has, in the previous chapter, been connected with the history of ideas flowing from Aristotle's treatise on time, Augustine's own restatement of Plotinus' position may itself appear as reflecting the concerns first voiced in Aristotle and offering his own, novel solution to the age-old dilemma of how to reconcile subjective and objective time. Of particular importance in this connection will be the problem of whether and to what extent Augustine's theory of time was linked with his attitude towards the existence of a universal soul which in the past has been controversially assessed.

There is, moreover, the question of whether Augustine's view had any forerunners among earlier Christian thinkers. This possibility has been emphatically

---

[1] Grandgeorge 1896, 75–80.

affirmed in a number of papers published by John F. Callahan.[2] Callahan, who had a lifetime interest in ancient theories of time,[3] advanced the view that Augustine's psychological theory of time was anticipated by a group of late fourth-century Christian thinkers, Basil the Great, his friend Gregory Nazianzen and Basil's younger brother, Gregory of Nyssa. All three hailed from Cappadocia, located in today's Turkey, and are therefore conventionally known as the three Cappadocian fathers. Callahan identified a 'psychological view' of time especially in Gregory of Nyssa[4] but also argued that a passage from Basil's first book *Against Eunomius*, written in the early 360s, served as a source for Augustine's reflections on time in his *Confessions*.[5]

These papers were authored in 1958 and 1960, respectively, so more than sixty years ago. Nevertheless, despite considerable interest in the Cappadocian concept of time in the meantime, they have found hardly any attention. Richard Sorabji briefly considered Callahan's argument only to dismiss it out of hand.[6] More recently, his views have been more sympathetically discussed by P. Tzamalikos who argued, however, that both the Cappadocians and Augustine depended on Origen while, at the same time, misrepresenting him to an extent.[7]

It may therefore be useful in the present context to reassess Callahan's case about what he called the 'psychological' nature of Gregory's theory of time before moving on to a consideration of Augustine's more famous views and their connection with the preceding intellectual tradition.

John F. Callahan and the psychological theory of time

There can be but little doubt that the principal approach to time in early Christian literature was cosmological and, more specifically, conditioned by the emergence of the Christian doctrine of creation.[8] Church fathers followed the Platonic tradition in juxtaposing time as a mark of creation with the atemporal eternity of God but pushed this logic even further. Insofar as God created the world from nothing (*ex nihilo*), traditional Greek ideas about the divinity of the cosmos

---

2 Callahan 1958a; 1958b; 1960.
3 Cf. also Callahan 1948; 1967.
4 Callahan 1960.
5 Callahan 1958b.
6 Sorabji 1983, 94–5.
7 Tzamalikos 2006, 227–8.
8 That this is the case for Origen is clear from the treatment in Tzamalikos 2006, part II. For studies in other fathers cf. Daniélou 1970; Otis 1976; Bradshaw 2006.

had to appear unacceptable to adherents of the new religion.[9] This affected the postulation of intermediate beings which had previously appeared attractive as bridging the metaphysical gulf between first principle and the material world. While ancient Christians were not opposed to the existence of spiritual realities, notably angels, these were ultimately classified as 'created' beings rather than standing halfway between the apex of ontological perfection and the messy world of our experience. They could not, therefore, serve as explanations for the origin of time in the way Plotinus' universal soul could.

There was initially one exception to this general rule in that the Logos, the pre-existent Christ, was often conceived as a point of transition from the absolute oneness of the Father towards the multiplicity of the created world.[10] This view, however, faced a fundamental crisis in the fourth century when, in response to the teaching of the Alexandrian presbyter Arius, the Church posited that the divine Trinity was *homoousios*, consubstantial, thus excluding any form of subordination among its members. It is clear from the ensuing controversy that those participating in the debate understood this doctrinal determination as sharpening the dichotomy between divine atemporality and eternity on the one hand and created timeliness on the other.[11]

This doctrinal framework was not, it seems, conducive to the kind of experiential approach to time we have found in Aristotle and which, arguably, found its expression in his claim that time could not exist without a soul that counts it. It is therefore understandable that Patristic views of time have seemed close to the more formal Stoic notion of time as an 'interval' (*diastema*) structuring the physical world, all the more since the two traditions shared the assumption of time as finite, stretching from a determinate beginning to an end point although only the Christians saw this single period as identical with the entire history of the world.[12]

And yet, an approach to Patristic views of time from a Stoic background merely evades the deepest problems faced by the early Christian authors. For the Stoics with their immanent, materialist interpretation of the physical world offered no answers to the kind of difficulties generated by the Christian juxtaposition of an eternal, transcendent God with a temporal creation. In this regard, rather, Christian authors found themselves in the company of the Platonic tradi-

---

9 Cf. for a poignant statement on this matter Dörrie 1987, 32. On the creation *ex nihilo* see May 1994; Blowers 2012, 167–84.
10 For this view in Origen see Zachhuber 2022.
11 Expressed in Gregory of Nyssa through the term *diastema*. Cf. Balás 1976; Verghese 1976.
12 See previous note. On the Stoic theory see Clark 1944, 340–1. Otis (1976, 336 n.1) sees 'no indication that the term [sc. *diastema*] came into Christian currency from Stoicism'.

tion, for better or worse. Like the Platonists, the early Christians had to come to terms with the objection that time, when primarily defined by its contrast with the perfection of divine eternity, is left unexplained in its empirical character. Plotinus' theory of time as the life of the universal soul was designed as a remedy to this very problem but relied on metaphysical assumptions that were not shared by the fathers. Their dichotomous ontology thus left early Christian thinkers with a 'negative' definition of time, but without the ontological resources of Neoplatonism that helped Plotinus towards a more positive, experiential account.

Callahan's thesis was, in brief, that precisely this state of affairs pushed Christian thinkers towards more psychological ideas about time. He writes of those who

> ... took the conception of time (of Plotinus, for example) as the creative live of a universal, divine principle of soul, and adapted it to a philosophical view that could not include such a principle in its explanation of nature and motion, referring time instead to the activity of another soul, the human. Time in such a context has a special relevance to the life of man, and the division of time into past and future is significant in terms of the psychological activities of memory and anticipation.[13]

Callahan then went on to give an impressive range of citations from Gregory of Nyssa's writings which illustrate his point. Gregory regularly refers to the contrast between created beings and God, especially in his controversy with Eunomius of Cyzicus, contrasting divine atemporality with creaturely existence in time. The latter is often described in existential or at least experiential terms. Past and future, Gregory writes, are 'affections' (*pathe*) of created beings in accordance with memory and anticipation.[14] Elsewhere we read that

> Human life moves in measurable time, and proceeds by advancing from a beginning to an end, and our life here is divided into past and future, the latter being expected, the former remembered.[15]

This experience of life as extended from past into the future is, undoubtedly, problematical. In his treatise *On the Soul and the Resurrection*, Gregory writes

---

13 Callahan 1960, 59.
14 Gregory of Nyssa, *Contra Eunomium* I 372 (GNO I 136, 22–4).
15 Gregory of Nyssa, *Contra Eunomium* II 459 (GNO I, 360, 17–21) ET: Hall 2007, 163: ἐπειδὴ γὰρ ἡ ἀνθρωπίνη ζωὴ διαστηματικῶς κινουμένη ἀπό τινος ἀρχῆς εἴς τι τέλος προϊοῦσα διέξεισι καὶ μεμέρισται πρὸς τὸ παρῳχηκός τε καὶ προσδοκώμενον ὁ τῇδε βίος, ὡς τὸ μὲν ἐλπίζεσθαι τὸ δὲ μνημονεύεσθαι.

of the struggle between memory and hope, the past and the future as the condition of human beings during their period of estrangement from the divine. Depending on human choices, the memories can be good or bad, but in any event, they are more emotionally powerful than our expectations for the future:

> [The human] soul is not affected in the same way towards what lies before it , as one may say, as to what it has left behind; for hope leads the forward movement, but it is memory that succeeds that movement when it has advanced to the attainment of the hope; and if it is to something intrinsically good that hope thus leads on the soul, the print that this exercise of the will leaves upon the memory is a bright one; but if hope has seduced the soul with some phantom only of the Good, and the excellent Way has been missed, then the memory that succeeds what has happened becomes shame, and an intestine war is thus waged in the soul between memory and hope, because the last has been such a bad leader of the will.[16]

Despite this tragic dimension of temporality, however, the existence of time is also providential. Time, Gregory can say, is measure because 'time is the measure of every particular thing that is measured. What takes place certainly takes place in time, and the period of time lasts just as long as every event lasts'.[17] As much, then, as Gregory thinks our temporal existence in the sequence of past, present, and future is a consequence of our distance from God, it is still, also, a sign of God's care for the needs of his creatures.

Richard Sorabji, as has already been mentioned, rejected Callahan's argument on the grounds that Gregory never identifies 'past and future with memory and expectation'.[18] This criticism is legitimate as far as it goes. There is no doubt that Gregory's overriding scheme remains cosmological; his theory of time is inscribed into his doctrine of creation. Time, for Gregory, is therefore not dependent on human awareness of time. He could never have agreed with Aristotle that

---

16 Gregory of Nyssa, *De anima et resurrectione* (GNO III/3, 67, 12–68, 2). ET: Moore/Wilson 1893, 449: οὐχ ὁμοίως τῆς ψυχῆς κατὰ τὸ ἔμπροσθεν αὐτῆς, ὡς ἂν εἴποι τις, καὶ τὸ ὀπίσω διακειμένης. Ἐλπὶς μὲν γὰρ καθηγεῖται τῆς ἐπὶ τὸ πρόσω κινήσεως, μνήμη δὲ δέχεται πρὸς τὴν ἐλπίδα προϊοῦσαν τὴν κίνησιν· ἀλλ' εἰ μὲν πρὸς τὸ φύσει καλὸν ἡ ἐλπὶς τὴν ψυχὴν ἄγοι, φαιδρὸν ἐνσημαίνεται τῇ μνήμῃ τὸ ἴχνος ἡ τῆς προαιρέσεως κίνησις· εἰ δὲ διαψευσθείη τοῦ κρείττονος, εἰδώλῳ τινὶ καλοῦ, παρασοφισαμένης τὴν ψυχὴν τῆς ἐλπίδος, ἡ ἐπακολουθοῦσα τοῖς γινομένοις μνήμη αἰσχύνη γίνεται. Καὶ ἐμφύλως οὗτος ὁ πόλεμος ἐν τῇ ψυχῇ συνίσταται, μαχομένης τῇ ἐλπίδι τῆς μνήμης, ὡς κακῶς καθηγησαμένης τῆς προαιρέσεως.
17 Gregory of Nyssa, *In ecclesiasten homiliae* (GNO V 376,23–377, 4). ET: Hall/Moriarty 1993, 102: χρόνος οὖν ἀντὶ τοῦ μέτρου ἡμῖν νενόηται, διότι παντὸς τοῦ καθ' ἕκαστον μετρου<μένου> ὁ χρόνος μέτρον ἐστίν. τὰ γὰρ γινόμενα ἐν χρόνῳ γίνεται πάντως, καὶ τῇ παρατάσει ἑκάστου τῶν γινομένων καὶ τὸ διάστημα τοῦ χρόνου συμπαρατείνεται.
18 Sorabji 1983, 95.

there might be no time without a soul insofar as time is created by God, and God is not (a) soul.

It is, however, possible to concede this point and yet retain the core of Callahan's thesis. In fact, Callahan himself observed that the creative power which Plotinus ascribed to the universal soul is not, in Gregory, transferred to the human person.[19] Yet the fact that the human soul in Gregory is quite obviously divested of the cosmological significance Soul had for Alexander, Plotinus, and Simplicius means that the psychological or, perhaps better, experiential character of time, which had been sidelined in some of those authors, moves more to the fore and thus, ironically, restores an important aspect of the original Aristotelian rationale for connecting time and soul.

It is remarkable that, for Gregory, it is human awareness of past and future more than the unchanging movements of the celestial spheres which offers the paradigm for the *diastemic* character of time. In this connection, Callahan is not without justification in referring to Gregory's anthropocentrism as conceptually important. The notion that humanity has been made 'in the image of God' (Gen. 1, 27) is pivotal for the thought of this church father who unambiguously explained this biblical expression in terms of the ontological relationship of the intelligibility of the human soul or mind to God.

It is therefore not far-fetched to take seriously Gregory's regular references to the human experience of an extension of time from past to future as indicative of a psychological or experiential turn in the theory of time that moves into the direction of the Augustinian theory, *even though* it is also important to see that neither Gregory of Nyssa nor any of his Cappadocian friends had the particular interest in introspection that was so typical for the bishop of Hippo. Absent this interest, however, the shift towards the subjective in Gregory's view is all the more telling because it indicates a particular inflection of the Neoplatonic viewpoint that occurred almost inevitably within Christianity. To have seen that remains the merit of Callahan's research from the middle of the twentieth century.

Augustine on time as the distention of the spirit

Augustine's reflections on time may today be the most celebrated among all ancient texts dealing with this topic. While Aristotle's theory is often heavily criticised, Augustine's ideas have proved attractive to a host of twentieth century

---

19 Callahan 1960, 63.

thinkers especially in the phenomenological tradition. Augustine has been an influence on Husserl and Heidegger as well as, later on, Paul Ricoeur.[20] Parallels between his account and the influential theory of time in the works of Henri Bergson have also been observed although the latter are not, apparently, due to literary influence.[21]

What makes Augustine unique among ancient authors may be described as his interest in and concern for the interiority of the human self primarily, inevitably, his own.[22] It is impossible to read the *Confessions*, arguably the pre-eminent testimony of this intellectual tendency without being struck by its nearly unique position within the literature of antiquity. Neither Plotinus nor Gregory of Nyssa display anything resembling this fascination for one's own interior even though they share in many ways Augustine's intellectual background.

A first explanation of Augustine's particular approach to the problem of time and soul would, then, have to point to the combination of intellectual *influences* on the one hand and the bishop's individuality on the other. As for the former, much of what has been discussed heretofore is once again pertinent. Like Gregory of Nyssa, Augustine initially inscribes time into the framework of the Christian doctrine of creation. Thus far, time is to him juxtaposed with God's eternity and atemporality.[23] Time is a cosmic, not a purely subjective reality, in that it is created by God; in fact, it came into existence together with the generation of the visible world, as he states in agreement with both the *Timaeus* and the Christian tradition.[24]

Furthermore, like Gregory, Augustine was impressed by the Neoplatonist account of time he could find in Plotinus. I leave to one side here the notorious problem of Augustine's *knowledge* of Greek philosophy and the paths through which it may have been mediated into his largely Latin intellectual cosmos.[25] I take it that, as demonstrated by L. Grandgeorge in his classical study, *St Augustin et le néo-platonisme*, Augustine's ideas on time and eternity were developed in conversation with Plotinus' *Ennead* III 7. From the parallels adduced by Grand-

---

20 Husserl 1966, 3; Heidegger 1927, 427–8; 2016; Ricoeur 1983, 21–65. Cf. Flasch 2016, 27–75; Herrmann 1992; Agustín Corti 2006; Coyne 2015. For further discussions on Augustine's view of time cf. Duchrow 1966 and Schmidt 1985.
21 Flasch 2016, 30.
22 On Augustine's 'invention of the inner self' cf. Cary 2000, interestingly without an extensive discussion of his theory of time.
23 Book XI of the *Confessions* itself begins with a lengthy discussion of God's eternity and his creation of time: *Confessiones* XI 1–12. Cf. Meijering 1979, 5–57; Flasch 2016, 289–94.
24 Augustine, *Confessiones* XI 14,17: *nullo ergo tempore non feceras aliquid, quia ipsum tempus tu feceras.*
25 Cf. e.g. Cary 2000, ch. 3.

george it is clear that Augustine was particularly impressed by Plotinus' argument that time had to be explained against the backdrop of eternity.²⁶

It is, then, plausible that Augustine, like his slightly older Greek peer, Gregory of Nyssa, was also impressed by Plotinus' positive account of time. In other words, Augustine like Gregory took from the Neoplatonist author a sense that the 'negative' time that was *not* eternity needed to be complemented by an account that explained time in its phenomenological or experiential reality. And like Gregory, Augustine realised that, in order to accomplish this task within a Christian context, he had to relocate this account in the soul or mind of the individual human person. These agreements cannot surprise, given especially the fact that Plotinus himself, notwithstanding his evident commitment to the universal soul as the ultimate origin of time, wrote about soul and time in a way that *could* (and still can) also be read as referring to the soul of individual human beings.²⁷

Be this as it may, it is at this point where Augustine's personal inclination comes into play. Whereas we have seen Gregory go hardly beyond vague and general references to the human experience of past and future, memory and expectation, Augustine clearly comes into his own when elaborating this very aspect of the problem. The reason is the specific problem from which Augustine starts. It has often been said that Augustine in Book XI of the *Confessions* addresses the question what time is. This is not wrong, of course, but in order to understand Augustine's approach it is crucial to see that to him the question what time is, is largely tantamount to the question of how we can know time. Yet Augustine's problem is not or not primarily epistemological. Rather, one could call it, in Kantian language, transcendental: what is the condition for the possibility of our knowledge of time? How can it be explained that we speak of time, that we quantify and measure it?²⁸

Scholars have observed echoes of philosophical scepticism in Augustine's account.²⁹ The bishop of Hippo was clearly conscious that the reality of our ideas about time and our use of temporal language do not in themselves prove the reality of time. In fact, he seems to concede that there are good reasons to be doubtful regarding our everyday references to longer and shorter periods of time. After all, to the extent that they refer to the past, they refer to something that no longer is there; to the extent that they refer to the future, they refer to

---

26 Grandgeorge 1896, 75–80.
27 Cf. Tempest-Walters 2019, 93–4.
28 Cf. e.g. Augustine, *Confessiones* XI 15, 18: *et tamen dicimus longum tempus et breve tempus, neque hoc nisi de praeterito aut futuro dicimus.*
29 Callahan 1967, 82–4. Meijering 1979, 58–9.

something that does not yet exist. If they finally, refer to the present they refer to something that does not seem to have an extension.[30]

This exposition of the problem is of crucial importance for understanding Augustine's particular interest in time and soul or mind.[31] It seems that, unless there is a justification for our belief that time exists in shorter or longer intervals, any cosmological or even theological answers will not be helpful. And the kind of justification that is needed, it seems, has to turn on the particular way in which our mind acquires consciousness of time.

Against the backdrop of the theories discussed in earlier parts of this book, it is notable how much emphasis Augustine places in this connection on the idea of time as measure. He is entirely with Aristotle in polemicising against the notion that time might *be* the movement of the celestial sphere.

> Do you [sc. God] command me to concur if someone says time is the movement of a physical entity? You do not. For I learn that no body can be moved except in time. You tell me so, but I do not learn that the actual movement of a body constitutes time. That is not what you tell me. For when a body is moved, it is by time that I measure the duration of the movement, from the moment it begins until it ends.[32]

There is no reason to think that Augustine had first-hand knowledge of the *Physics*, but as we have seen, Plotinus' theory too was, despite appearances, indebted to the intellectual concerns underlying the Aristotelian theory; Augustine may simply have adapted the view he found there to his own needs.[33] In any event, however, the agreement is remarkable and signals a joint concern across the centuries in identifying time as something that cannot simply be the same as physical reality be it bodies or their movement. Rather, time needs consciousness, it is inseparable from a being with an awareness of time.

What precisely this means, however, is a point on which Augustine has learnt to go beyond Aristotle. Awareness of time is tied to a kind of being that has temporality, a structure designed to know and understand time. Being an intellect in itself, as Aristotle's reference to the mind that is counting time might

---

30 Augustine, *Confessiones* XI 15,18–20.
31 Augustine in this text makes apparently no distinction between *animus* and *anima*.
32 Augustine, *Confessions* XI 24, 31, ET: Chadwick 1991, 256: *iubes ut approbem, si quis dicat tempus esse motum corporis? non iubes. nam corpus nullum nisi in tempore moveri audio: tu dicis. ipsum autem corporis motum tempus esse non audio: non tu dicis. cum enim movetur corpus, tempore metior quamdiu moveatur, ex quo moveri incipit donec desinat.* Cf. Callahan 1958b who here compares Basil of Caesarea's *Adversus Eunomium* I 21 where this view is ascribed to Eunomius.
33 Cf. Meijering 1979, 86: 'Hier steht Augustin, [... Aristoteles] näher, als oft angenommen wird.'

seem to imply, is not enough. Instead, a special type of intellect is needed, one specifically adapted to this mode of existence by means of its own temporality. This, Plotinus had argued, was the case for the universal soul (although the latter was not in time, it had life and thus a proto-temporal structure), whereas Augustine seeks to ground temporality in the created mind of human beings whose ability to remember the past and anticipate the future allows them to know all dimensions of time at any given moment.

A further aspect is important in marking the radicalness of Augustine's break from the pre-Christian tradition. In rejecting the idea that time is celestial movement, the church father includes a swipe against the normativity of the heavenly revolutions that would have sounded sacrilegious to earlier Greek thinkers:

> If the heavenly bodies were to cease and a potter's wheel were revolving, would there be no time by which we could measure its gyrations, and say that its revolutions were equal; or if at one time it moved more slowly and at another time faster, that some rotations took longer, others less? And when we utter these words do not we also speak in time? In our words some syllables are long, others short, in that the sounding of the former requires a longer time, whereas the latter are shorter. [...] There are stars and heavenly luminaries to be 'for signs and for times, and for days and for years' (Gen. 1: 14).[34]

It had seemed self-evident to the entire Greek tradition, to Plato and Aristotle as well as Alexander and Plotinus, that the regularity of celestial movements was the paradigm of temporality, a meeting-point of time and eternity. This assumption was taken for granted regardless of whether individual thinkers saw time as identical with these movements (some early Platonists) or distinct from them (Aristotle, Plotinus). To Augustine, however, these movements are contingent on God's creative agency. By signifying the course of days, months, and years, they fulfil a practical function in accordance with God's command revealed to us in the Book of Genesis. Augustine is here engaged in disenchantment – his reference to the potter's wheel is evidently provocative. It is, then, arguable that the specific import given to human temporality is a by-product of his devaluation of cosmic order.

---

34 Augustine, *Confessiones* XI 23, 29. ET: Chadwick 1991, 254–5: *si cessarent caeli lumina et moveretur rota figuli, non esset tempus quo metiremur eos gyros et diceremus aut aequalibus morulis agi, aut si alias tardius, alias velocius moveretur, alios magis diuturnos esse, alios minus? aut cum haec diceremus, non et nos in tempore loqueremur aut essent in verbis nostris aliae longae syllabae, aliae breves, nisi quia illae longiore tempore sonuissent, istae breviore? [...] sunt sidera et luminaria caeli 'in signis et in temporibus et in diebus et in annis'.*

All these factors must be taken into consideration when seeking to interpret Augustine's famous thesis that time is nothing but the 'distention of the mind'.³⁵ There is, I would argue, no radical discontinuity with the Aristotelian idea that time cannot exist without soul as both thinkers approach time from the problem of the measurement of movement. Augustine, one might say, intends both more and less than what previous readers have found in Aristotle's *aporia*. He says more in that, for him, the dependence of time on soul needs temporality and not merely intellectuality to be explained. He says less, however, insofar as Augustine's soul or mind has no physical role in bringing about cosmic movement and thus in generating time.

The latter aspect seems to reopen the problem from which the earlier history of interpreting Aristotle's *aporia* took its starting point. Does not a definition of time simply in relation to the individual person's memories and their anticipation of the future make time entirely subjective? Bertrand Russell gave stark expression to this criticism. According to him, Augustine 'was content to substitute subjective time for the time of history and physics':

> Memory, perception, and expectation, according to him, made up all that there is of time. But obviously this won't do. All his memories and all his expectations occurred at about the time of the fall of Rome, whereas mine occur at about the time of the fall of industrial civilisation, which formed no part of the Bishop of Hippo's expectations. Subjective time might suffice for a solipsist of the moment, but not for a man who believes in a real past and future, even if only his own.³⁶

Whatever objections may be raised against the form in which Russell presents his claim including the 'positivist' premises on which it is based, it is hard to deny that *prima facie* he touches on a real problem. Is not an approach to time that begins with introspection, as is the case with Augustine's, struggling to explain (1) the intersubjective identity of this experience and (2) the universal, cosmic unity of time? Plotinus, who shared a similar approach, was apparently worried about this very difficulty; his stipulation of universal soul as prefiguring the human experience of time is arguably at least partly driven by this kind of concern.³⁷

As for Augustine, there are at least two questions that ought to be treated separately. The first is whether his theory could ever be called 'subjective'

---

35 Augustine, *Confessiones* XI 26, 33: *inde mihi visum est nihil esse aliud tempus quam distentionem; sed cuius rei, nescio, et mirum, si non ipsius animi*.
36 Russell, 2009, 187–8.
37 In the universal soul all human souls are one: cf. Caluori 2015, 17–25.

given how clearly he grounds the existence of time in the doctrine of creation. Throughout much of book eleven of the *Confessions*, in fact, theological problems with this doctrine are at the forefront of his enquiry including his attempt to rebut the Manicheans' mocking objection that it left unexplained what God did before he created the world.[38] Even where he enters into his reflections on time as distention of the mind, he continues the dialogue with God, so central to *Confessions* as a whole. The charge of 'solipsism' thus far seems off the mark.

It may seem, however, that Augustine should perhaps not be let 'off the hook' so easily. There is, admittedly, no doubt that the author of the *Confessions* is no longer truly troubled by scepticism but has accepted faith in the Christian God. His reflections are thus, 'faith seeking understanding' to use an Augustinian phrase today associated with the eleventh-century theologian, Anselm of Canterbury. And yet, this theological certainty still leaves him with the question of what time is. He clearly does not think he can simply deduce a legitimate answer from his theistic convictions. Nor – and perhaps more to the point – does he choose to move directly from the acceptance of divine creation to a cosmological account of time; in fact, as we have seen he seems rather reserved towards such an approach.

Augustine, then, cannot be so easily absolved from the need to explain how his account of time ensures its universality. This gives rise to the second question, namely, whether Augustine does not, in fact, need the kind of universal soul or mind accepted in various forms by Alexander of Aphrodisias, Plotinus, and Simplicius and imputed by them to Aristotle as well. This question has been raised in previous scholarship, and it is therefore now necessary to consider it in some more detail.

Augustine's theory of time and the universal soul

In recent decades, two eminent scholars of Augustine's thought have argued that the bishop's theory of time only works if his account of the temporal structure of the individual mind is ultimately grounded in an analogously structured universal or cosmic soul or mind. The two scholars, Kurt Flasch and Robert Teske, have thus applied to Augustine the kind of logic we saw ancient readers apply to Aristotle.[39] And as the ancient readers of the Stagirite, these modern researchers

---

38 Augustine, *Confessiones* XI 10, 12. Cf. Meijering 1979, 40 on the historical background.
39 Flasch 2016, esp. 223–8; Teske 1983. For a critical assessment of their attempt cf. Bettetini 2001, 46.

have sought to bolster their claim by observing that Augustine throughout his oeuvre seemed willing to at least toy with the existence of a universal soul.

In fact, Teske builds his case with the help of an initial overview of Augustine's references to the world soul, especially in some of his early works. Quite characteristic is the following statement from his early work (387/8) *The Greatness of the Soul* (*De quantitate animae*).[40] It responds to the question of how many souls there are which Augustine admits he finds hard to answer:

> For if I should tell you that there is only one soul, you will be at sea because of the fact that in one it is happy, in another unhappy; and one and the same thing cannot be happy and unhappy at the same time. If I should say that it is one and many at the same time, you will smile; and I would not find it easy to make you suppress your smile. But if I say simply that it is many, I shall have to laugh at myself, and it will be harder for me to suffer my own disapprobation than yours.[41]

Despite Augustine's evident reserve towards all three answers, it seems clear that he distinguishes them for more than rhetorical effect. The first one ('there is only one soul') is clearly wrong, but whereas the second one ('it is one and many at the same time') seems merely hard to convey to his addressee, Evodius, Augustine would feel embarrassed to hold to the third one ('it is many'). Augustine thus seems inclined to think that the soul is one and many although he refrains from making this idea a topic of instruction in the present context.

Although Teske and some others have, in this connection, referred to the 'world soul', it is immediately clear that the doctrine to which Augustine felt somewhat attracted is not the idea found in the *Timaeus* and many Platonic authors from the imperial period according to which there is a soul that has the cosmos as its body, but Plotinus' concept of the universal soul in which all individual souls (including, incidentally, the world soul) are contained and embraced.[42] It is, admittedly, the case that Augustine in some passages also pondered the question of whether the world was an animal and, as such, had a soul.[43] In his *Retractions*, he offered some self-critical reflections on this topic:

---

[40] On the date cf. Colleran 1964, 4.
[41] Augustine, *De quantitate animae* 32, 69. ET: Colleran 1964, 97: *Si enim dixero unam esse animam, conturbaberis, quod in altero beata est, in altero misera; nec una res simul et beata et misera potest esse. Si unam simul et multas dicam esse, ridebis; nec mihi facile, unde tuum risum comprimam, suppetit. Sin multas tantummodo esse dixero, ipse me ridebo, minusque me mihi displicentem, quam tibi, perferam.*
[42] On the difference between the two cf. Caluori 2015, 22–5.
[43] Teske 1983, 76–7.

his earlier references to this doctrine had been 'said in utter rashness'⁴⁴ for, while Plato and others had asserted that the world was an animal, he himself had been 'unable to discover this by certain reason or know that the authority of Scripture proves it'.⁴⁵

A similar disavowal of the possibility that a universal soul exists in which all individual souls are contained does not seem to exist, however. Teske has, therefore, proposed that Augustine continues to be open to the existence of a universal soul at the time of the *Confessions*.⁴⁶ For this he has cited the following passage, which stands near the end of book XI and thus the conclusion of Augustine's reflections on time:

> Certainly if there were a mind endowed with such great knowledge and prescience that all things past and future could be known in the way I know a very familiar psalm, this mind would be utterly miraculous and amazing to the point of inducing awe. From such a mind nothing of the past would be hidden, nor anything of what remaining ages have in store, just as I have full knowledge of the psalm I sing. I know by heart what and how much of it has passed since the beginning, and what and how much remains until the end.⁴⁷

This great mind, Augustine subsequently emphasises, would nevertheless fall far below the perfection of God who knows past and future in a 'much more wonderful and much more mysterious way' namely, in an entirely atemporal manner. He is, then, speculating about a created being which, nevertheless, is ontologically exalted beyond the status of human beings. According to Teske, Augustine is here hinting at a Christianised version of Plotinus' universal soul which helps him avoid the kind of conceptual problems to which Russell and others have pointed. In other words, Augustine implicitly recognised the need for a trans-individual consciousness as the basis of temporality, and he gestured at the existence of such a being although he did not explicitly commit to it.⁴⁸

---

44 Augustine, *Retractationes* I 5, 3: *hoc totum prorsus temere dictum est*. Cf. Teske 1983, 77
45 Augustine, *Retractationes* I 11 4: *Sed animal esse istum mundum, sicut Plato sensit aliique philosophi plurimi, nec ratione certa indagare potui, nec divinarum Scripturarum auctoritate persuaderi posse cognovi*. Cf. Teske 1983, 78)
46 Teske 1983, 79–80.
47 Augustine, *Confessiones* Augustin, XI 31, 41: *certe si est tam grandi scientia et praescientia pollens animus, cui cuncta praeterita et futura ita nota sint, sicut mihi unum canticum notissimum, nimium mirabilis est animus iste atque ad horrorem stupendus, quippe quem ita non lateat quidquid peractum et quidquid relicum saeculorum est, quemadmodum me non latet cantantem illud canticum, quid et quantum eius abierit ab exordio, quid et quantum restet ad finem*. ET: Chadwick 1991, 261.
48 Teske 1983, 90–2. Cf. Flasch 2016, 404–13.

How far can this text support the line of argument advanced by Teske? Let us begin by asking what kind of being the Bishop of Hippo is here proposing. It is not, arguably, the angelic host and thus, probably, no mere shorthand for the non-material creation in general.[49] As a matter of fact, Augustine's vague and speculative language would seem to suggest that he is *not* thinking of any being whose existence the Christian tradition has generally affirmed. What he has in mind is, rather a creature that may or may not exist from the point of view of someone committed to the Catholic worldview. Thus far, Teske is right in connecting the statement with Augustine's earlier statements about the universal soul which seemed to indicate that he considered such a being neither mandated nor excluded by Christian teaching.

As soon as the possibility is taken seriously that the *animus* of which Augustine writes here is either Plato's world soul or Plotinus' universal soul, however, differences abound. First of all, there is no trace in these lines of the idea of a soul of the world that has the cosmos as its body and explains how it changes and how it forms an integrated unity. Augustine is thus far removed from either Platonic or Stoic notions of a world soul.

Yet the present passage does no address either the problem of the unity of all souls. Augustine does not say or imply that the great mind about which he speculates here is the totality of all souls or that his or any individual soul is a part of this universal mind. In fact, he does not describe the relationship between the temporality of this mighty mind and our minds in terms of participation at all but merely in terms of pre-eminence. The postulation of a mind 'abounding in knowledge and foreknowledge' does not explain how our own awareness of time is possible but what *perfect* temporality would be.

To this end, the bishop describes a mind that would be able to perform the integration of past, present, and future into a single time at the universal level. Such a mind would not simply be aware of 'some' past and 'some' future; 'whatever is past and whatever is yet to come would [not] be concealed from' such a being. Nevertheless, its sense of time would be analogous to our temporality. Its universal awareness of past and future would be more perfect but in principle comparable to Augustine's own experience when chanting a psalm whose 'past and future' is not 'hidden from me' while singing it: 'how much of it had been sung from the beginning and how much still remained till the end'.

All this makes the mind to which Augustine here refers rather different from Plotinus' universal soul. The latter, as we have seen, was not temporal but, so to speak, proto-temporal; it possessed a structure, which Plotinus called 'life' and

---

49 So rightly Teske 1983, 90.

which prefigured human temporality. Augustine's knowledgeable mind, by contrast, seems to have temporality that is in principle like our own although the evidence is not entirely clear. Augustine admittedly introduces the whole passage with a reference to a possible 'creature above time', but he then refers to the temporality of 'that spirit' in language that suggests an existential experience of memories of the past and the expectation of the future rather like that encountered by human beings.

If Augustine, then, was not here merely offering a 'thought-experiment', as some have suggested,[50] but considered the existence of such a mind a serious possibility, his conceptual purpose in doing so was rather different from that we encountered in Plotinus. Not only is the mighty mind not the originator of time – this arguably would go without saying – there is also no indication that this *animus* is meant to guarantee intersubjective validity to our awareness of time by representing a Soul in which individual consciousnesses participate.

Perhaps Augustine was worried about the kind of objection we have encountered in Bertrand Russell that is, the limitation and contingency of individual memories and expectations. A mind with unlimited knowledge of past and future events could, it seems, respond to the charge that universal time could not be constituted on the basis of any person's memories and hopes. Such a proposal would, in any event, be an extension of Augustine's own argument rather than a return to Platonic or Neoplatonic ideas.

It is, however, doubtful that Augustine had any such purpose in mind in writing the present passage. As the context makes clear, his overriding concern was with God's atemporality. This he sought to affirm in order decisively to defeat the Manichean objection to the Christian doctrine of creation. All *aporiae* regarding this theory go away, Augustine suggests, once we fully grasp the radicalness of God's eternity. The introduction of the great mind merely reinforces this point. The text thus needs to be read from its conclusion:

> But far be it from you, Creator of the universe, creator of souls and bodies, far be it from you to know all future and past events in this kind of sense. You know them in a much more wonderful and much more mysterious way. A person singing to a song he knows well suffers a distension or stretching in feeling and in sense-perception from the expectation of future sounds and the memory of past sound. With you it is otherwise. You are unchangeably eternal, that is the truly eternal Creator of minds. Just as you knew heaven and earth in the beginning without that bringing any variation into your knowing, so you made heaven

---

[50] Fischer 1998, 322.

and earth in the beginning without that meaning a tension between past and future in your activity.[51]

While the great mind would be 'utterly miraculous and amazing', to Augustine it ultimately only proves how much more miraculous and amazing God himself is whose relationship to time stands in fundamental dichotomy to even the most perfect among created beings.

While it must therefore remain open whether Augustine believed such a mind existed, there is no indication in the text that he felt that such a being had to be postulated to fortify his notion of time as distention of the mind or even that he believed that his subjective theory was in and of itself in need of such an extension. This, of course, brings back the question of whether Augustine *should have* adopted a universal principle of temporality. Is it the case, as Kurt Flasch in particular has urged, that without such an additional assumption Augustine's theory of time falls flat? This question will be addressed in the final section of the present chapter.

Time and soul in Augustine: an assessment

It may be useful at this point to return once again to the scholarship of John F. Callahan. As he saw it, there was a simple, genetic explanation for the emergence of what he called the 'psychological' account of time in Gregory of Nyssa and subsequently in Augustine. According to this theory, the Christian theories started from Plotinus' localisation of time in the universal soul but, since they had no place for such a Soul in their Christian metaphysics, they transposed the 'temporality' into the human soul or mind and thus created the novel concept of psychological time.

This now seems like a plausible overall narrative. Both Gregory and Augustine, we need to recall, begin and end with the notion that time is made by God as part of his creation of the world. The specific purpose of the Plotinian Soul, then, namely, to explain the origin of temporality from an ontological source that on principle was unconnected with time, was no longer needed within

---

51 Augustine, *Confessions* XI 31, 41, ET: Chadwick 1991, 261–2: *longe tu, longe mirabilius longeque secretius. neque enim sicut nota cantantis notumve canticum audientis expectatione vocum futurarum et memoria praeteritarum variatur affectus sensusque distenditur, ita tibi aliquid accidit incommutabiliter aeterno, hoc est vere aeterno creatori mentium. sicut ergo nosti in principio caelum et terram sine varietate notitiae tuae, ita fecisti in principio caelum et terram sine distentione actionis tuae.*

the theistic context of the early church fathers. The existence of *diastema* or *distensio* did not need its own ontological carrier to be explained. This left the subjective or epistemic side of the phenomenon; and this aspect, it seems, gained comparatively more attention.

One can, admittedly, ask whether such a reconstruction is not making things look simpler than they were. The very notion of a 'theistic' context that in itself explains the origin of temporality from an entirely atemporal God may be more paradoxical – or may have appeared more paradoxical to ancient Christian thinkers – than such a neat expression seems to suggest. We have evidence, for example, that Gregory of Nyssa saw the problem of how an intelligible God could have created material being as hard to solve; in fact, his explanation was that there was no matter and that creation as a whole should be seen as composed of intelligible components which only in their combination make up what we call materiality. Overall, the transition from God's simplicity and unity into the plurality and diversity of the world seems to have been as puzzling to Greek Patristic thinkers as to their Platonic peers. In order for the problem to disappear, a strong emphasis on divine omnipotence is needed which, while sometimes asserted in the Fathers, does not seem to have been universally accepted by them.

As for Augustine, we have seen how the possibility that the human soul ought to have a more universal counterpart within created reality loomed large at least in his earlier writings. It would therefore seem rash to ascribe to him an unmitigated sense that the postulation of the Christian God as creator of 'heaven and earth' suddenly made superfluous the need of a hierarchical ontological structure within created being.

Despite this kind of qualification, however, the kernel of Callahan's thesis remains intact in that the removal of Plotinus' universal soul as a metaphysical principle of temporality explains the novel concern for human temporality as the subjective basis of time. This coincidence in Gregory and Augustine, notwithstanding some considerable differences, is remarkable and supports the conclusions Callahan had wanted to draw from his findings.

In view of the longer narrative which this book has followed, this result is furthermore interesting in that it represents continuity as well as innovation. We have seen how close Augustine can be, in places, to the language of Aristotle's treatise on time. In fact, it is arguable that Aristotle's interest in the experiential dimension of time comes in these Christian authors to an unexpected novel appreciation. As such, it undoubtedly appears in revised form. The soul 'counting' time as number in *Physics* IV 14 and Augustine's temporally structured, 'distented' soul are not simply identical concepts. Yet there are important, underlying agreements between the two which deserve to be noted without occluding differences.

These similarities are all the more notable in view of the rather different trajectory on which we have found the later Neoplatonic tradition. Simplicius, while seeming to affirm Aristotle's teaching to the letter, divested his theory of any trace of a subjective or experiential dimension. The soul, whether as cause of change or whether as 'counting' change ultimately is the universal soul, the cosmic soul. The reality of time as experienced by human beings thus appears pushed to the margins of philosophical reflection.

It is, then, not without irony that the criticism directed against Aristotle by some of his readers can be turned against an author such as Augustine as well. Does not the emphasis on the subjective approach to time, its experiential basis, and the conceptual need for the human soul or mind to exist as the basis of temporality fail to account for the universality and the cosmic dimension of time? It is intriguing to observe that in both authors, Aristotle as well as Augustine, there are hints at additional theoretical assumptions that might help with this problem, but not an explicit embrace of those theories. This reluctance could well be due to their realisation that more far-reaching theoretical constructions will inevitably lead attention away from the experiential and phenomenal basis of time to a metaphysical and cosmological speculation about its transcendent source.

Conclusion

The present study has had the purpose of investigating ancient ideas about the relationship between cosmic or 'objective' time and the conscious awareness of time. This problem, which continues to be debated into our own time then took the shape of a discussion about the relationship between time and soul. Throughout the period studied, this relationship was seen as complex and problematic, and it is this fact that constitutes the abiding value of this discussion.

The investigation has covered extensive historical ground, from the classical period to the end of late antiquity. The main thread of the discussion was provided by Aristotle's *aporia*, in *Physics* IV 14, regarding the relationship between time and soul. For some authors, this text was the starting point of their own discussions, for others it was an idea they commented on or criticised. Yet others developed ideas about time and soul without textual dependence on Aristotle's text.

Aristotle's theory of time has been variously interpreted. While a full appreciation of his view was beyond the remit of this investigation, it has been argued that the *aporia* according to which time as number could not exist without a soul that counts it is not an obscure addendum to an otherwise rather different, naturalistic theory, but rather a plausible extension of an approach to time which seeks to understand it as neither identical with the phenomena of the natural world nor categorically detached from them. As much as Aristotle pushes against Plato's notion that time should be understood from its relationship with eternity, as much does he oppose the simple identification of time with movement.

The *aporia* was understood throughout antiquity as advancing the claim that time could not exist without soul. No evidence was found for the later interpretation, held among others by Thomas Aquinas, according to which Aristotle had meant to suggest that time could exist perfectly well without soul. On the basis of this *prima facie* reading, later philosophers gave a variety of responses to the Aristotelian puzzle.

Writing in the first century BCE, Boethus of Sidon could still roundly dismiss Aristotle's case on the basis that cosmic time evidently exists independently of the human soul. In Boethus there is no hint, at least not an explicit one, that the soul might be a universal, cosmic soul rather than the individual one of a human person. But even if he reckoned with such an interpretation, as some scholars have argued, he clearly rejected such a theory as well.

Two centuries later, Alexander of Aphrodisias, the major commentator of the Peripatetic school, found himself in a different position. It is clear that he did not see it as an option simply to reject an opinion found in Aristotle. That said, his defence of the co-dependency of time and soul, as it can be reconstructed from a variety of sources, is clearly based on more than an act of reverence towards the Stagirite.

Already his 'dialectical' argument against Boethus, namely, that we ought to distinguish between the possibility that something countable could exist without someone counting on the one hand and something countable existing *as* countable on the other, is far from trivial. The commentator insists in an almost hermeneutical manner on the irreducibility of the awareness of time for its existence *as time without* falling into an idealist identification of the cosmos with our idea of it.

Yet it was his inclusion of the broader cosmological dimension of the relationship of time and soul which constituted the most original aspect of Alexander's discussion. In a bold move, he drew on the non-Aristotelian tradition of a world soul to argue that without such a soul no movement was possible and thus no time. Aristotle's claim that time cannot exist without soul was, then, defended against the charge of idealism on the grounds that 'soul' has both an individual and a cosmic dimension.

Quite how Alexander thought about the relationship between the two is not entirely clear from the fragmentary remains of his writing, but the most plausible assumption is that he believed they were connected in such a way that the soul's cosmic function as causing celestial movements, and its *noetic* function of counting time could be seen as belonging together.

Despite Alexander's use of a theory Aristotle himself had rejected, it is arguable that his interpretation of the relationship of time and soul comes closest to doing justice to the intuition behind Aristotle's own argument and, especially, his *aporia*. Alexander's Aristotle is unafraid of adopting Platonic ideas to avoid a naturalist viewpoint that would have made the *aporia* appear, in Richard Sorabji's words, 'a silly mistake'.[1] At the same time, Alexander does *not* turn the universal or cosmic soul into the true subject of time thus retaining Aristotle's insistence on the close relationship of time and (physical) change.

A crucial turning point was reached in Plotinus' *Ennead* III 7. While his references to Aristotle were largely dismissive and often elliptical, the brief consideration that could in the present book be given to this important text showed that the relationship of Plotinus' ideas to the Aristotelian tradition was much more substantial than those explicit references would suggest. In grounding time in Soul, Plotinus took a step which, despite his evident overall indebtedness

---

[1] Sorabji 1983, 90.

to the *Timaeus*, cannot really be derived from this background or indeed from any previous Platonic author.

This makes the obvious parallels with Aristotelian ideas, especially as found in Alexander of Aphrodisias, particularly significant. It seems that Alexander and Plotinus agreed on the importance of soul, including universal soul, for time. This is not to say that they agreed *tout court*. Rather, Plotinus sought to re-establish Plato's view that time can only be properly conceived from the perspective of eternity. At this point, his difference from the Aristotelian standpoint is radical.

Yet it seemed that Plotinus was aware of the problem in Plato to which the Aristotelian tradition pointed and which I have here referred to as a 'negative' conception of time, that is, time defined merely by its contrast with eternity. Plotinus' exposition of time as correlated with the universal soul shows his attempt to mitigate this downside of the Platonic account. Especially his references to the relationship between time and the human experience of fallenness indicate his awareness of the need to retain an experiential account of time while adopting an overall Platonic framework.

This awareness, however, was subsequently lost in the erudite commentary Simplicius wrote on Aristotle's *Physics*. His account, it has been argued, despite its attempt fully to validate Aristotle's own theory alongside Alexander's interpretation, aligned time with universal soul in such a way that no room appeared to be left for the subjective, experiential dimension of temporality. While fully affirming the co-dependency of both on each other, Simplicius' Neoplatonic account in fact reduces this dependency to a cosmic and ontological one with little or no reference to individual awareness or experience of time.

The development from Plotinus to Simplicius put into relief, finally, the rather different intellectual development among some Christian thinkers. A brief consideration of Gregory of Nyssa and a more detailed examination of Augustine's ideas have suggested understanding those thinkers, too, against the backdrop of Plotinus' restatement of the relationship of time and soul. The Christian authors, it appears, found it natural to adopt the Platonic view that understands time from its contrast with divine eternity. In fact, this contrast was even more strongly cast in the Christian, theistic view with its uncompromising juxtaposition of God and world. Time is primarily God's creation and, as such, radically different from the world's uncreated origin. This meant that the Christian view was even more strongly threatened by the 'negative' conception of time. At the same time, the seemingly elegant solution adopted by Alexander and Plotinus, to connect time with a cosmic soul was in principle excluded by Christian thinkers.

This constellation led, as John F. Callahan has argued half a century ago, to the innovative adoption of a more subjective, experiential focus than had existed in earlier authors. In Gregory and especially in Augustine we find an unprecedented emphasis on time as correlated with the human experience of temporality. In Gregory, this emphasis is expressed through regular references to memory and hope as dimensions of human existence in time. In Augustine, we encounter an impressively worked out theory of time as the *distention of the mind* or soul.

This development, inevitably, raises the question of whether the theory enunciated by these Christian authors, especially Augustine, represents a satisfactory account of time. Does it not lack the universal dimension of soul that would explain the intersubjective validity of time? Is the theory not, therefore, in the final reckoning, purely subjective and, as such, incapable of explaining time as both experiential and cosmic? Augustine, to be sure, would have countered this charge with the observation that the universal dimension of time was implied by his account of creation which, even in Book XI of the *Confessions* foregrounds and frames the later exposition of time as distention of the soul. At the same time, his own text seems to support the suspicion that the dogmatic statement about the origin of time in God's creative act cannot in and of itself explain the reality of human temporality.

Against those who have argued that Augustine's theory would have been more successful had he affirmed a world soul as the subject of cosmic time, it needs to be recalled how easy it was for this kind of theory to lose its experiential basis in the subject. The world soul, after all, was part of the cosmic order, and as such hardly the answer to the problem of time as experienced by human beings.

One cannot, therefore, conclude that antiquity has solved the problem of the relationship between cosmic and experiential time. It has, however, configured it in a fascinating variety of ways. Studying the various authors who have contributed to this debate over the centuries helps understand the intricate and complex nature of the question. In the twentieth century, J. M. E. McTaggart argued that the tension between the notion of time as flowing from future to present to past on the one hand (A Series) and that of a sequence of moments whose positions vis-à-vis each other never change (B Series), cannot to resolved; it therefore indicates that time is unreal.[2] It is intriguing to note that the possibility that time is unreal was also addressed and taken seriously by Aristotle and Augustine. Whatever the merit of their own answers, their efforts show that any attempt

---

2 McTaggart 1908.

to 'save the phenomenon' of time cannot avoid addressing the difficulties amply discussed in the centuries between these two great thinkers.

Bibliography

Primary Sources

Aristotle, *Physica*, ed. W. D. Ross. Oxford: OUP, 1936
Aristotle, *De caelo*, ed. P. Moreaux. Paris: Les Belles Lettres, 1965.
Aristotle, *Metaphysica*, ed. Werner Jaeger. Oxford: OUP, 1957.
Aristotle, *Categoriae*, ed. Lorenzo Minio-Paluello. Oxford: OUP, 1949.
Aristotle, *De anima* ed. W. D. Ross. Oxford: OUP, 1961
Atticus, *Fragmenta*, ed. E. des Places. Paris: Les Belles Lettres, 1977.
Augustine, *Confessiones*, ed. James J. O'Donnell. Oxford: OUP, 1992.
Augustine, *De quantitate animae*, ed. W. Hörmann (CSEL 89). Vienna: Verlag der österreichischen Akademie der Wissenschaften, 1986.
Augustine, *Retractationes*, ed. P. Knöll (CSEL 36). Vienna: Verlag der österreichischen Akademie der Wissenschaften, 1902.
Basil of Caesarea, *Adversus Eunomium*, edd. Louis Doutreleau/George-Matthieu de Durand/Bernard Sesboüé (SC 305). Paris: Éditions du Cerf, 1982–3.
Empedocles, *Fragmenta*, edd. H. Diels/W. Kranz, *Die Fragmente der Vorsokratiker*, vol. 1, 6th edn. Berlin: Weidmann, 1951, 308–74.
Gregory of Nyssa, *Contra Eunomium* I-III, ed. Werner Jaeger, 2 vols, 2nd edn. (GNO I-II). Leiden: Brill, 1960.
Gregory of Nyssa, *De anima et resurrectione*, ed. Andreas Spira (GNO III/3). Leiden: Brill, 2014.
Gregory of Nyssa, *In ecclesiasten homiliae*, ed. P. J. Alexander (GNO V). Leiden: Brill, 1962.
Homer, *Odyssea*, ed. P. von der Mühll. Basel: Helbing & Lichtenhahn, 1962.
Plato, *Phaedrus*, ed. J. Burnet, *Platonis Opera*, vol. 2. Oxford: Clarendon Press, 1901.
Plato, *Timaeus*, ed. J. Burnet, *Platonis Opera*, vol. 4. Oxford: Clarendon Press, 1902.
Plato, *Leges*, ed. J. Burnet, *Platonis Opera*, vol. 5. Oxford: Clarendon Press, 1907.
(Ps.-)Plato, *Definitiones*, J. Burnet, *Platonis Opera*, vol. 5. Oxford: Clarendon Press, 1907.
Plotinus, *Enneades*, edd. Paul Henry/Hans-Rudolf Schwyzer, *Plotini Opera*, 3 vols. Oxford: Clarendon Press, 1964–82.
Porphyry, *Vita Plotini*, edd. Paul Henry/Hans-Rudolf Schwyzer, *Plotini Opera*, vol. 1. Oxford: Clarendon Press, 1964.
Simplicius, *In Aristotelis physicorum libros commentaria*, ed. H. Diels, 2 vols (CAG IX-X). Berlin: Reimer 1882–1895.
Themistius, *In Aristotelis physica paraphrasis*, ed. H. Schenkl (CAG V/2). Berlin: Reimer, 1900.
Themistius, *In libros Aristotelis de anima paraphrasis*, ed. R. Heinze (CAG V/3). Berlin: Reimer, 1899.
Themistius, *In Aristotelis metaphysicorum librum Λ paraphrasis*, ed. S. Landauer (CAG V/5). Berlin: Reimer 1903.

Secondary Literature

Agustín Corti, C. (2006), *Zeitproblematik bei Martin Heidegger und Augustinus*. Würzburg: Königshausen & Neumann.
Annas, Julia (1975), 'Aristotle, Number and Time', *The Philosophical Quarterly* 25, 97–113.
Balaudé, Jean-François and Francis Wolff (2005), *Aristote et la pensée du temps* (Le temps philosophique). Paris: Université Paris X – Nanterre.
Balaś, David (1976), 'Eternity and Time in Gregory of Nyssa's *Contra Eunomium*', in: Heinrich Dörrie, Margarete Altenburger, Ute Schramm (eds.), *Gregor von Nyssa und die Philosophie: Zweites internationales Kolloquium über Gregor von Nyssa. Freckenhorst bei Münster 18–23. September 1972*. Leiden: Brill, 128–53.
Baltussen, Han (2008), *Philosophy and Exegesis in Simplicius: The Methodology of a Commentator*. London: Bloomsbury.
Barney, Rachel (2009), 'Simplicius: Commentary, Harmony, and Authority', *Antiquorum Philosophia* 3, 101–19.
Beierwaltes, Werner (1967), *Plotin: Über Ewigkeit und Zeit (Enneade III 7)*. Frankfurt/M.: Klostermann.
Betegh, Gábor (2010), 'The Transmission of Ancient Wisdom: Texts, doxographies, libraries', in: Lloyd P. Gerson (ed.), *History of Philosophy in Late Antiquity*, vol. 1. Cambridge: CUP, 25–38.
Bettetini, Maria (2001), 'Measuring in accordance with *dimensiones certae*: Augustine of Hippo and the question of time', in: P. Porro (ed.), *The Medieval Concept of Time: Studies on the Scholastic Debate and its Reception in Early Modern Philosophy*. Leiden: Brill, 33–53.
Blowers, Paul M. (2012), *Drama of the Divine Economy: Creator and Creation in Early Christian Theology and Piety*. Oxford: OUP.
Bostock, David (2006), *Space, Time, Matter, and Form: Essays on Aristotle's Physics*. Oxford: OUP.
Bradshaw, David (2006), 'Time and Eternity in the Greek Fathers', *The Tomist* 70, 311–66.
Broadie, Sarah (2011), *Nature and the Divine in Plato's Timaeus*. Cambridge: Cambridge University Press.
Callahan, John Francis (1948), *Four Views of Time in Ancient Philosophy*. Cambridge, MA: Harvard University Press.
Callahan, John Francis (1958a), 'Greek Philosophy and the Cappadocian Cosmology', in: *Dumbarton Oaks Papers* 12, 29–57.
Callahan, John Francis (1958b), 'Basil of Caesarea a New Source for St Augustine's Theory of Time', in: *Harvard Studies in Classical Philology* 63, 437–54.
Callahan, John Francis (1960), 'Gregory of Nyssa and the Psychological View of Time', in: *Atti des XII Congresso Internazionale di Filosofia* 11, 59–66.
Callahan, John Francis (1967), *Augustine and the Greek Philosophers*. New York, NY: Villanova University Press.
Caluori, Damian (2015), *Plotinus on Soul*. Cambridge: CUP.
Carter, Jason W. (2017), 'Aristotle's Critique of Timaean Psychology', *Rhizomata* 5, 51–78.
Cary, Phillip, *Augustine's Invention of the Inner Self: The Legacy of a Christian Platonist*. Oxford: OUP.
Chadwick, Henry (1991), *Saint Augustine: Confessions. Translated with an Introduction and Notes*. Oxford: OUP.

Chiaradonna, Riccardo (2013), 'Platonist Approaches to Aristotle: from Antiochus of Ascalon to Eudorus of Alexandria (and beyond)', in: Malcolm Schofield (ed.), *Aristotle, Plato and Pythagoreanism in the First Century BC*. Cambridge: CUP, 28–52.

Chiaradonna, Riccardo and Rashed, Marwan (eds.) (2020), *Boéthos de Sidon: Exégète d'Aristote et philosophe* (Commentaria in Aristotelem Graeca et Byzantina, 1). Berlin: de Gruyter.

Clark, Gordon H. (1944), 'The Theory of Time in Plotinus', *The Philosophical Review* 53/4, 337–58.

Colleran, Joseph M. (1964), *St. Augustine: The Greatness of the Soul. The Teacher. Translated and Annotated*. Westminster, MD: The Newman Press.

Coope, Ursula (2005), *Time for Aristotle: Physics IV 10–14* (Oxford Aristotle Studies). Oxford: OUP.

Cornford, Francis Macdonald (1937), *Plato's Cosmology*, London: Routledge & Kegan Paul.

Coyne, Ryan (2015), *Heidegger's Confessions: The Remains of St Augustine in 'Being and Time' and Beyond*. Chicago: Chicago University Press.

Curd, P. (1998), *The Legacy of Parmenides: Eleatic Monism and Later Presocratic Thought*, Princeton, NJ: Princeton University Press.

Daniélou, Jean (1970), *L'être et le temps chez Grégoire de Nysse*. Leiden: Brill.

Detel, Wolfgang (2021), *Subjektive und objektive Zeit: Aristoteles und die moderne Zeit-Theorie*. Berlin: de Gruyter.

Deuse, Werner (1983), *Untersuchungen zur mittel- und neuplatonischen Seelenlehre*. Wiesbaden: Franz Steiner.

Dillon, John M. (1996), *The Middle Platonists. 80 B.C. to A.D. 220*, 2nd revised ed. Ithaca, NY: Cornell University Press.

Dörrie, Heinrich (1987), *Die geschichtlichen Wurzeln des Platonismus. Bausteine 1–35: Text, Übersetzung, Kommentar*, ed. Annemarie Dörrie (Der Platonismus in der Antike. Grundlagen – System – Entwicklung, 1). Stuttgart-Bad Cannstatt: Fromman-Holzboog.

Duchrow, Ulrich (1966), 'Der sogenannte psychologische Zeitbegriff Augustins im Verhältnis zur physikalischen und geschichtlichen Zeit', in: *Zeitschrift für Theologie und Kirche* 63, 267–88.

Edwards, Mark (2019), *Aristotle and Early Christian Thought*. London: Routledge.

Fischer, N. (1998), '"Kostbar ist mir jeder Tropfen Zeit...": Einführung zum elften Buch von Augustins "Confessiones"', in: *Theologie und Glaube* (1998) Heft 88, 304–23.

Flasch, Kurt (2016), *Was ist Zeit? Augustinus von Hippo. Das XI. Buch der Confessiones. Historisch-philologische Studie. Text – Übersetzung – Kommentar* (Rote Reihe, 13), 3rd edn. Stuttgart: Klostermann, 2016.

Frede, Dorothea (2017), 'Alexander of Aphrodisias', in: *Stanford Encyclopedia of Philosophy*, electronic resource. Accessed on 7 January 2022. https://plato.stanford.edu/entries/alexander-aphrodisias/.

Frede, Michael (1987a), 'The Title, Unity, and Authenticity of the Aristotelian *Categories*', in: Id., *Essays in Ancient Philosophy*. Minneapolis, MN: Minnesota University Press, 11–28.

Frede, Michael (1987b), 'Individuals in Aristotle', in: Id., *Essays in Ancient Philosophy*. Minneapolis, MN: Minnesota University Press, 1987, 49–71.

Goldschmidt, Victor (1953), *Le système stoïcien et l'idée de temps*. Paris: Vrin, 1953.

Goldschmidt, Victor (1982), *Temps physique et temps tragique chez Aristote: Commentaire sur le quatrième livre de la Physique (10–14) et sur la Poétique*. Paris: Vrin.

Grandgeorge, L. (1896), Saint Augustin et le Néo-Platonisme, Paris: Leroux.
Griffin, Michael J. (2015), *Aristotle's Categories in the Early Roman Empire*. Oxford: OUP.
Hackforth, R. (1936), 'Plato's Theism', *The Classical Quarterly* 30, 4–9.
Hadot, Ilsetraut (1987), 'La vie et l'oeuvre de Simplicius d'après des sources grecques et arabes', in: ead., *Simplicius: Sa vie, son oeuvre, sa survie: Actes du colloque international de Paris (28 Sept. – 1er Oct. 1985)*. Berlin: de Gruyter, 3–39.
Hadot, Ilsetraut (2015), *Athenian and Alexandrian Neoplatonism and the Harmonization of Plato and Aristotle*, trans. Michael Chase (Studies in Platonism, Neoplatonism, and the Platonic Tradition, 18). Leiden: Brill.
Hall, Stuart/Moriarty, Rachel (1993), 'Gregory, Bishop of Nyssa: Homilies on Ecclesiastes', in: id. (ed.), *Gregory of Nyssa: Homilies on Ecclesiastes. An English Version with Supporting Studies. Proceedings of the Seventh International Colloquium of Gregory of Nyssa (St Andrews, 5–10 September 1990)*. Berlin: de Gruyter, 31–144.
Hall, Stuart (2007), 'The Second Book against Eunomius: Translation', in: Lenka Karfíková, Stoc Douglass and Johannes Zachhuber (eds.), *Gregory of Nyssa: Contra Eunomium II. An English Version with Supporting Studies. Proceedings of the 10th International Colloquium on Gregory of Nyssa (Olomouc, September 15–18, 2004)*. Leiden: Brill, 59–201.
Harry, Chelsea C. (2015), *Chronos in Aristotle's Physics: On the Nature of Time*. Cham: Springer.
Heidegger, Martin (1927), *Sein und Zeit*. Halle: Niemeyer.
Heidegger, Martin (2016), 'Augustinus: Quid est tempus? Confessiones lib. XI (Vortrag in Beuron 26. Oktober 1930)', in: id. *Gesamtausgabe*, vol. 80/1, ed. G. Neumann. Frankfurt/M: Klostermann, 2016, 429–56.
Helmig, Christoph (ed.) (2020), *World Soul – Anima Mundi: On the Origins and Fortunes of a Fundamental Idea*. Berlin: de Gruyter.
Herrmann, Friedrich Wilhelm von (1992), *Augustinus und die phänomenologische Frage nach der Zeit*. Frankfurt/M.: Klostermann.
Huby, Pamela F. (1981), 'An Excerpt from Boethus of Sidon's Commentary on the *Categories*?' in: *The Classical Quarterly* 31, 398–409.
Husserl, Edmund (1966), *Vorlesungen zur Phänomenologie des inneren Zeitbewusstseins*, ed. Rudolf Boehm (Husserliana, 10). Den Haag: Nijhoff.
Hussey, Edward (1983), *Aristotle. Physics, Books III and IV: Translated with Introduction and Notes*, Oxford: Clarendon Press.
Jeck, Udo Reinhold (1994), *Aristoteles contra Augustinum: Zur Frage nach dem Verhältnis von Zeit und Seele bei den antiken Aristoteleskommentatoren, im arabischen Aristotelismus und im 13. Jahrhundert* (Bochumer Studien zur Philosophie, 21). Amsterdam: Grüner.
Johansen, Thomas (2009), 'From Plato's Timaeus to Aristotle's De Caelo: The Case of the Missing World Soul', in: Alan Bowen and Christian Wildberg (eds.): *New Perspectives on Aristotle's De Caelo*. Leiden: Brill, 9–28.
Karamanolis, George (2006), *Plato and Aristotle in Agreement? Platonists on Aristotle from Antiochus to Porphyry* (Oxford Philosophical Monographs). Oxford: OUP.
Köckert, Charlotte (2009), *Christliche Kosmologie und kaiserzeitliche Philosophie. Die Auslegung des Schöpfungsberichtes bei Origenes, Basilius und Gregor von Nyssa vor dem Hintergrund kaiserzeitlicher Timaeus-Interpretationen*. Tübingen: Mohr Siebeck.

Kupreeva, Inna (2010), 'Alexander of Aphrodisias on Form: A Discussion of Marwan Rashed, *Essentialisme*', in: *Oxford Studies in Ancient Philosophy* 38, 211–49.

Lehoux, David (2017), *Creatures born of Mud and Slime: The Wonder and Complexity of Spontaneous Generation*. Baltimore, MD: Johns-Hopkins University Press.

Magrin, Sara (2016), 'Plotinus' Reception of Aristotle', in: Andrea Falcon (ed.), *Brill's Companion to the Reception of Aristotle in Antiquity* (Brill's Companions to Classical Reception 7). Leiden: Brill, 258–76.

Marrou, Henri-Irenée (1958), *Saint Augustin et la fin de la culture antique*, 4th edn. Paris: Boccard.

May, Gerhard (1994), *Creatio ex Nihilo: The Doctrine of 'Creation out of Nothing' in Early Christian Thought*, trans. A. S. Worrall. London: T & T Clark.

McGuire, J.E./Strange, Steven (1988), 'An Annotated Translation of Plotinus *Ennead* iii 7: On Eternity and Time', *Ancient Philosophy* 8, 251–71.

McTaggart, J. M. E. (1908), 'The Unreality of Time', in: *Mind* 17, 457–73.

Meijering, E. P. (1979), *Augustin über Schöpfung, Ewigkeit und Zeit: Das elfte Buch der Bekenntnisse*. Leiden: Brill.

Menn, Stephen (1995), *Plato on God as Nous*. Carbondale, IL: Southern Illinois University Press.

Mesquita, Antonio Pedro (2018), Review of: Chelsea Harris, *Chronos in Aristotle's Physics: On the Nature of Time*, *Ancient Philosophy* 38, 460–6.

Meyrav, Yoav (2016), 'Spontaneous Generation and its Metaphysics in Themistius' Paraphrase of Aristotle's *Metaphysics* 12', in: Richard Sorabji (ed.), *Aristotle Re-interpreted: New Findings on Seven Hundred Years of Ancient Commentators*. London: Bloomsbury, 195–210.

Meyrav, Yoav (2020), *Themistius: On Aristotle's Metaphysics 12* (London: Bloomsbury).

Moraux, Paul (1973–2001), *Der Aristotelismus bei den Griechen*, 3 vols. (Peripatoi: Philologisch-historische Studien zum Aristotelismus, 5–7/1). Berlin: de Gruyter.

Moreau, Joseph (1939), *L'âme du monde de Platon aux stoïciens*, Paris: Les Belles Lettres.

Moreschini, Claudio (1987), 'Attico: una figure singolare del medioplatonismo', in: Wolfgang Haase (ed.), *Aufstieg und Niedergang der römischen Welt* II 36, 1. Berlin: De Gruyter, 477–91.

Moore, William/Wilson, Henry Austin (1893), *Select Writings and Letters of Gregory, Bishop of Nyssa. Translated with Prolegomena, Notes, and Indices* (A Select Library of Nicene and Post-Nicene Fathers, 5). London: Parker & Company.

Otis, Brooks (1976), 'Gregory of Nyssa and the Cappadocian Concept of Time', in: *Studia Patristica* 14, 327–57.

Palmer, John (2020), 'Parmenides', in: *Stanford Encyclopedia of Philosophy*, electronic resource. Accessed on 13 January 2022. https://plato.stanford.edu/entries/parmenides/#OveParPoe.

Rashed, Marwan (2007), *Essentialisme: Alexandre d'Aphrodise entre logique, physique et cosmologie* (Commentaria in Aristotelem Graeca et Byzantine, 2). Berlin: de Gruyter.

Rashed, Marwan (2011), *Alexandre d'Aphrodise: Commentaire perdu à la* Physique *d'Aristote (Livres IV–VIII). Les scholies byzantines* (Commentaria in Aristotelem Graeca et Byzantina. Quellen und Studien, 1). Berlin: de Gruyter.

Rashed, Marwan (2013), 'Boethus Aristotelian Ontology', in: Malcolm Schofield (ed.), *Aristotle, Plato and Pythagoreanism in the First Century BC*. Cambridge: CUP, 53–77.

Reinhardt, Tobias (2007), 'Andronicus of Rhodes and Boethus of Sidon on Aristotle's *Categories*', in: Robert W. Sharples and Richard Sorabji (eds.), *Greek and Roman Philosophy. 100 BC – 200 AD*, vol. 2 (Bulletin of the Institute of Classical Studies Supplement 94). London: Institute of Classical Studies, 513–29.

Reydams-Schils, Gretchen (1999), *Demiurge and Providence: Stoic and Platonist Readings of Plato's Timaeus*. Turnhout: Brepols.

Ricoeur, Paul (1983), *Temps et récit*, vol. 1: *L'intrigue et le récit historique*. Paris: Éditions du Seuil.

Rist, John (1969), *Stoic Philosophy*. Cambridge: Cambridge University Press.

Roark, Tony (2013), *Aristotle on Time: A Study on the Physics*. Cambridge: CUP.

Salles, Ricardo (2021), 'The Stoic World Soul and the Theory of Seminal Principles', in: James Wilberding (ed.), *World Soul: A History*. Oxford: OUP, 44–66.

Russell, Bertrand (2009), *Human Knowledge: Its scope and limits. With an introduction by John G. Slater*. London Routledge.

Sattler, Barbara and Richard D. Mohr (eds.) (2010), *One Book, The Whole Universe: Plato's Timaeus Today*. Las Vegas: Parmenides Publishing.

Schmidt, Ernst A. (1985), *Zeit und Geschichte bei Augustin* (Sitzungsberichte der Heidelberger Akademie der Wissenschaften). Heidelberg: Carl Winter.

Sharples, Robert William (1982), 'Alexander of Aphrodisias on Time', *Phronesis* 27, 58–81.

Sharples, Robert William (2007), 'Aristotle's Exoteric and Esoteric Works: Summaries and Commentaries', in: Id. and Richard Sorabji (eds.), *Greek and Roman Philosophy. 100 BC – 200 AD*, vol. 2 (Bulletin of the Institute of Classical Studies Supplement 94). London: Institute of Classical Studies, 505–12.

Sharples, Robert William (2008), 'Habent Sua Fata Libelli: Aristotle's *Cagegories* in the First Century BC', in: *Acta Antiqua Academiae Scientiarum Hungaricae* 48, 273–87.

Simesen de Bielke, Martín (2017), 'De la aporía del tiempo y el alma a la temporalidad del Dasein', *Rivista de Filosofía Diánoia* 62 (2017), 165–93.

Sonderegger, Erwin (1982), *Über die Zeit: Ein Kommentar zum Corollarium de tempore*. Göttingen: Vandenhoeck & Ruprecht.

Sorabji, Richard (1983), *Time, Creation and the Continuum*. London: Duckworth.

Striowski, Andra (2016), *Aristotle on Time and Soul*, PhD dissertation, University of Ottawa.

Tempest-Walters, Kit (2019), *A Translation of and Commentary on Plotinus' Ennead III.7 with an Interpretative Essay*, PhD dissertation, Royal Holloway, University of London.

Teske, Roland (1983), 'The World-Soul and Time in St Augustine', in: *Augustinian Studies* 14, 75–92.

Todd, Robert B. (1996), *Themistius: On Aristotle On the Soul*. London: Bloomsbury.

Tzamalikos, Panayiotis (1991), 'Origen and the Stoic View of Time', in: *Journal of the History of Ideas* 52, 535–61.

Tzamalikos, Panayiotis (2006), *Origen: Cosmology and Ontology of Time*. Leiden: Brill.

Urmson, J. O. (1992), *Simplicius: On Aristotle Physics 4.1–5.10–14*. London: Bloomsbury.

Urmson, J. O. (1992a), *Simplicius: Corollaries on Place and Time*. London: Bloomsbury.

Verghese, T. Paul (1976), 'Διάστημα and διάστασις in Gregory of Nyssa', in: Heinrich Dörrie, Margarete Altenburger, Ute Schramm (eds.), *Gregor von Nyssa und die Philosophie: Zweites internationales Kolloquium über Gregor von Nyssa. Freckenhorst bei Münster 18–23. September 1972*. Leiden: Brill, 243–60.

Wilberding, James (ed.) (2021), *World Soul: A History*. Oxford: OUP.

Wilberding, James (2021a), 'The World Soul in the Platonic Tradition', in: id., *World Soul: A History*. Oxford: OUP, 15–43.
Wright, M. R. et al. (eds.) (2000), *Reason and Necessity: Essays on Plato's Timaeus*. Swansea: Classical Press of Wales.
Zachhuber, Johannes (2004), 'Weltseele', in: Joachim Ritter, Karlfried Gründer and Gottfried Gabriel (eds.), *Historisches Wörterbuch der Philosophie*, vol. 12. Basel: Schwabe, 516–21.
Zachhuber, Johannes (2016), 'Physis', in: *Reallexikon für Antike und Christentum*, vol. 16 (Stuttgart: Hiersemann), 744–81.
Zachhuber, Johannes (2020), 'World Soul and Celestial Heat: Platonic and Aristotelian Ideas in the History of Natural Philosophy', in: Christoph Helmig (ed.), *World Soul – Anima Mundi: On the Origins and Fortunes of a Fundamental Idea*. Berlin: de Gruyter, 335–53.

General Index

academy (*See under* Platonic Academy)
active principle (in Stoicism)   38
agreement of Plato and Aristotle   6, 30
Alexander of Aphrodisias   29–36, 40–48, 52–4, 56–61, 63, 68, 72, 74, 82–4
– *Commentary on Aristotle's Physics*   31, 34, 40, 44, 57
– *Scholia* on the *Commentary on Aristotle's Physics*   31, 34–5, 40, 57
– *De tempore*   31, 34–5, 40
Alexandria   47, 54, 65
Andronicus of Rhodes   22–3, 27
angels, the angelic host   65, 77
Anselm of Canterbury   74
anticipation   66
Arabic reception of Greek philosophy   7, 16, 30, 43
Aristotle
– *Categories*   23–5, 27–8
– *Metaphysics*   19, 23–5, 42–3, 48
– *On the Heavens*   37
– *On the Soul*   19, 37
– *Poetics*   19
– *Physics*   3, 7, 10–21, 41–2, 50, 52–3, 82
Arius of Alexandria   65
Athens   22, 47, 54
Augustine   2–5, 7–9, 63–4, 68–81, 85
– *Confessions*   64, 69–74, 76, 79, 85
– *The Greatness of the Soul*   75
– *Retractions*   75–6
– the 'great mind'   76–9

Basil the Great   64, 71
– *Against Eunomius*   64
Bergson, Henri   69
Big Bang, the   1
Boethus of Sidon   22–9, 31, 33–5, 38, 45–6, 51–2, 57–60, 82–3
– *Commentary on the Categories*   23

Callahan, John F.   64–8, 79–80, 85
Caracalla   29

change   10–8, 24, 32–3, 41, 44–5, 49–50, 58–61
Chiaradonna, Riccardo   26, 28
Christian theology   4
commentaries   5, 8, 48, 53–4
Coope, Ursula   16, 18–9
cosmic soul (*See under* world soul)
cosmos   1, 12, 36–8, 43, 61, 64, 75, 77, 83
– as animal/living being   3, 36, 38, 75–6
– *kosmos noêtos*   49
Craftsman (Demiurge)   12, 36–7, 39
creation   2–3, 36, 39, 64–5, 74, 79–80, 85,
– doctrine of creation   64, 67, 69, 74, 78
– *creatio ex nihilo*   64

desire   35, 40–1
Diels, Hermann   56

Epicureans   6
eternity   12, 20, 49–50, 64–6, 69–70, 72, 78, 82, 84
Eunomius of Cyzicus   66
Evodius   75
experience, experiential   2, 4, 11, 19–20, 34, 36, 45–6, 53, 63, 65–6, 68, 70, 73, 77–8, 81

fixed stars   1, 19, 55
Flasch, Kurt   74, 79
form (in Aristotle)   11, 24
Form of the Good   38
forms (in Plato)   12, 36–8, 42
future, the   1, 2, 13, 66–8, 70, 72–3, 76–9, 85

God   2, 64–6, 67–9, 72, 74, 76, 78–80, 84–5
– divine omnipotence (*See under* omnipotence, divine)
– secondary gods   42–3
Grandgeorge, L.   69–70
Gregory of Nazianzus   64

Gregory of Nyssa 64–70, 79–80
– *On the Soul and the Resurrection* 66–7

Harry, Chelsea 16
heavenly movements, revolutions 12, 28, 38–9, 40–1, 44, 68, 71–2, 83
Heidegger, Martin 2, 16, 69
heterodox Aristotelianism 30
history 1, 65, 73
homoousios 65
Husserl, Edmund 69
hylomorphism 11

Ibn Rushd (Averroes) 43
intellect 16–7, 20, 40, 50

Justinian I 54

late antiquity 3–5, 8, 19, 30, 47, 82
logic 23
Logos (pre-existent Christ) 65
Lyceum 10, 23

Manichean, Manicheans 74, 78
Marrou, Henri-Irenée 8
matter 11, 24, 80
McTaggart, J.M.E. 85
measure 14, 50–1, 53, 56, 59, 67, 71–2
measurement 1–2, 28, 73
memory 66–67, 70, 73, 78, 85
Mesquita, António Pedro 16
Meyrav, Yoav 43
Middle Ages 3, 30
mind (*See also* intellect) 1–3, 14–5, 19–20, 35–6, 40–1, 70–4, 76–9
– distention of the mind (*See under* time)
Moraux, Paul 26, 60
movement (*See also* celestial movement) 1, 11–2, 35, 37–41, 45, 50, 67–8, 71–3, 82–3

nature (*See under physis*, nature)
Neoplatonists, Neoplatonic, Neoplatonism 4, 6, 30–1, 47–62, 69–70, 78, 81
number that counts/is counted 15, 19, 27

omnipotence, divine 80

ontology, ontological 2, 23–5, 33–4, 37, 45, 50, 58, 60–1, 66, 68, 79–80, 84
ontological perfection 65

paradigm 12, 37, 61, 68, 72
Parmenides 10–1
past, the 1–2, 13, 66–8, 70, 72–3, 76–9, 85
perception 1, 15, 25, 27, 46, 73
– sense-perception 78
Peripatetics, Peripatetic, Peripatos 4, 6, 8, 22–46, 48, 51–2, 61, 82
physis, nature 10–1, 13, 37, 42, 66
Plato 6–7, 11–2, 30, 38–9, 42–4, 48, 49–50, 60, 72, 76, 82, 84
– *Laws* 39
– *Sophist* 37
– *Timaeus* 3, 12, 36–9, 43, 45, 49, 69, 75, 84
Platonic Academy 10, 54
Platonist, Platonic, Platonism 4, 6, 20, 28–9, 30, 34, 37–8, 45–7, 50, 64–6, 72, 75, 78–8, 83–4
Plotinus 44, 48–53, 55–6, 59–61, 63, 65, 68–80, 83–4
– *On Time and Eternity* (*Ennead* III 7) 49–52, 55, 61, 69, 83
Porphyry 31, 48–9
present, the 2, 13, 67, 71, 77
Presocratics 7, 54
prime mover (*See under* unmoved mover)

Rashed, Marwan 24, 26, 28, 33, 44
reason (*logos*) 38
relation 33
Ricoeur, Paul 19, 69
Roark, Tony 16
Russell, Bertrand 73, 76, 78

Scepticism 70, 74
schools
– philosophical 4–6, 30
– Hellenistic 8, 54
secondary gods (*See under* God)
sensible reality 50
Septimus Severus 29

General Index

Simplicius of Cilicia   7, 25–6, 31, 47, 54, 68, 74, 81, 84
- *Commentary on Aristotle's Physics*   31, 34, 54–62, 84
- *Corollary on Time*   55–6
something (*ti*) (Stoicism)   39
Sorabji, Richard   17, 64, 67, 83
soul (*See also* world soul)
- rational soul (*See also* mind, intellect)   17, 41
- soul of the earth   42–4
- soul as
  - counting time   16–9, 25–7, 31–3, 40–1, 51–2, 56, 59–61, 71, 80–1
  - hypostasis   50, 60
  - principle of becoming   59–60
  - self-moving   37–9, 41

spirit (*pneuma*)   38
spontaneous generation   42–3
Stoic, Stoics, Stoicism   4, 6, 28, 30, 38–9, 47–8, 65, 77
sun   1, 35, 41–5

teleology   11
temporality   2–3, 19, 50–1, 67, 71–3, 76–81, 84
Teske, Robert   74–7
Themistius   25–6, 28, 42–4
- *Paraphrase of Aristotle's Metaphysics XII*   42–3
- *Paraphrase of Aristotle's Physics*   28
Thomas Aquinas   82
time
- awareness, consciousness of   1, 13, 18–9, 21, 34, 67–8, 71, 76–8, 82–4
- before and after structure   13, 16–8, 32–3, 58, 60
- first time (*prōtos chronos*)   55–6
- moment, now   13–5, 19
- negative definition of   66, 70, 84
- psychological theory of   64–8, 79
- reality of   1, 45, 70, 81
- substrate of   32–3, 58
- time as
  - cyclical   1
  - distention of the mind   2, 68–74, 79, 85
  - enumerated number   31, 58–60
  - extension of changeable being   59
  - image of eternity   12, 45, 49
  - interval (*diastema*)   39, 65
  - life of the soul   50, 56
  - number   14–5, 17, 27, 40–1, 53, 59–61, 80
  - objective   1, 2, 4, 7, 20, 28, 36, 46, 63, 82
  - psychological   50, 79
  - subjective   3–4, 45–6, 53, 63, 73
  - unidirectional   1
transition   10, 65, 80
Tzamalikos, P.   64

Urmson, J. O.   56

world, *see under* cosmos
world soul, cosmic soul   3–4, 34–46, 75–6, 82–3
- and universal Soul in Plotinus   50
- as found in
  - Alexander of Aphrodisias   34–6, 40–1
  - Augustine   75–6
  - Boethus   28
  - Plato   36–8
  - Simplicius   56–7
  - Stoics   38
  - Themistius   42–3

Index of Ancient Sources

Alexander of Aphrodisias
– *In physica*
  – IV 14   32–3
  – fr. 203   35, 40
– *De tempore*
  – § 16   35

Aristotle
– *Physica*
  – II 2   41
  – IV 11   12–5, 27
  – IV 12   53
  – IV 14   3, 16, 25, 32, 40
  – VIII 5–6   19
– *De caelo*
  – B 1   38
– *Metaphysica*
  – Γ 5   25
  – Z 3   24
  – Λ 3   42
  – Λ 7   40
  – Λ 8   19
  – Λ 12   42
– *Categoriae*
  – 2   24
– *De anima*
  – A 3   37
  – Γ 5   19

Atticus
– *Fragmenta*
  – 8   38

Augustine
– *Confessiones*
  – XI 10, 12   74
  – XI 14, 17   2
  – XI 15, 18   70
  – XI 15, 18–20   71
  – XI 23, 29   72
  – XI 24, 31   71
  – XI 26, 33   73
  – XI 31, 41   76, 79

– *De quantitate animae*
  – 32, 69   75
– *Retractationes*
  – I 5, 3   76
  – I 11, 4   76

Basil of Caesarea
– *Adversus Eunomium*
  – I 21   71

Boethos
– *Fragmenta*
  – 18   24
  – 36–7   24
  – 37 b   18, 25
  – 38a   26

Empedocles
– *Fragmenta*
  – B 8   10

Gregory of Nyssa
– *Contra Eunomium*
  – I 375   66
  – II 459   66
– *De anima et resurrectione*, ed. Spira
  – p. 67, 12–68, 2   67
– *In ecclesiasten homiliae*, ed. Alexander
  – p. 376, 23–377, 4   67

Homer
– *Odyssea*
  – X 303   10

Plato
– *Phaedrus*
  – 245c   60
– *Timaeus*
  – 30 b4-c1   3, 36
  – 35 a   37
  – 36 e-37 c   37
  – 37c 38 c   39
  – 37 d5   12

   – 39d 12
– *Leges*
   – X 896 a 39

(Ps.-) Plato
– *Definitiones*
   – 411 b 12

Plotinus
– *Enneades*
   – III 7,1,16 – 7 49
   – III 7,9,1 50, 59
   – III 7,9,78 – 84 51
   – III 7,11,15 – 20 52
   – III 7,11,20 50
   – III 7,11,44 – 5 50
   – III 7, 13,16 – 8 52
   – IV 4 44

Porphyry
– *Vita Plotini*
   – 5 49
   – 14 48

Simplicius
– *In Aristotelis physicorum libros commentaria, ed. Diels*
   – p. 738, 2 – 5 59

   – p. 758, 30 – 759, 16 57
   – p. 759, 14 – 7 57
   – p. 759, 19 – 20 31
   – p. 759, 21 58
   – p. 759, 21 – 8 32
   – p. 759, 29 – 30 32
   – p. 759, 31 – 760, 3 33
   – p. 760, 12 – 3 58
   – p. 760, 14 – 26 57
   – p. 760, 18 58
   – p. 760, 27 – 30 58
   – p. 760, 32 59
   – p. 761, 5 – 8 60
   – p. 790, 26 – 31 55
   – p. 792, 21 – 3 55
   – p. 792, 26 – 31 56

Themistius
– *In Aristotelis physica paraphrasis, ed. Schenkl*
   – p. 163, 7 – 18 28
– *In libros Aristotelis de anima paraphrasis, ed. Heinze*
   – p. 26, 25 – 30 43
– *In Aristotelis metaphysicorum librum Λ paraphrasis*
   – ו, 2-ח , 28 42

www.ingramcontent.com/pod-product-compliance
Lightning Source LLC
Chambersburg PA
CBHW071823230426
43670CB00013B/2549